SAS AND ELITE FORCES GUIDE
MANHUNT

D0097033

SAS AND ELITE FORCES GUIDE
MANHUNT

THE ART AND SCIENCE OF TRACKING HIGH PROFILE ENEMY TARGETS

ALEXANDER STILWELL

LYONS PRESS
Guilford, Connecticut
An imprint of Globe Pequot Press

Copyright © 2012 Amber Books Ltd
All illustrations © Amber Books Ltd
Published by Amber Books Ltd (www.amberbooks.co.uk)

This Lyons Press edition first published in 2012

Lyons Press is an imprint of Globe Pequot Press.

Library of Congress Cataloging-in-Publication Data is available on file.

ISBN: 978-0-7627-8017-4

Project Editor: Sarah Uttridge
Designer: Zoë Mellors
Illustrations: Julian Baker

Printed in Singapore

10 9 8 7 6 5 4 3 2 1

CONTENTS

CASE STUDY 1:

The Greatest Manhunt in History – Finding Bin Laden:
Part 1

It was the greatest terrorist crime in history and its mastermind – Osama bin Laden – became the most wanted and the most hunted man in history.

On 11 September 2001, Islamic terrorists, some of them trained as commercial airline pilots, hijacked four US airliners on routine flights. Two were crashed into the twin towers of the World Trade Center, one into the Pentagon and one crashed in a field. The brave men and women of the New York rescue services and police went into the twin towers to attempt to control the blaze and rescue survivors. Due to the calamitous impact of the aircraft upon the structure of the buildings, however, 343 firefighters and 23 policemen themselves died as they collapsed.

It did not take long for the US Government to identify the perpetrators of this attack, and Osama bin Laden and al-Qaeda were equally quick to claim credit.

The United Nations Security Council passed Resolution 1368 (2001) in which it called on 'all States to work together urgently to bring to justice the perpetrators, organizers and sponsors of these terrorist attacks' and also stressed 'that those responsible for aiding, supporting or harbouring the perpetrators, organizers and sponsors of these acts will be held accountable'.

The die was cast. Now it was just a question of finding Osama bin Laden and his allies.

Terrorist Lair

Al-Qaeda, which translated from Arabic means 'The Base', was founded by Osama bin Laden in the late 1980s. The roots of the terrorist organization lay in the insurgency against Soviet forces that had occupied Afghanistan between 1979 and 1989. The Taliban regime took control in Afghanistan from about 1996 and imposed their

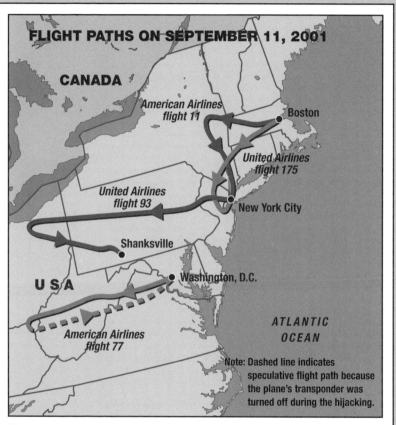

FLIGHT PATHS ON SEPTEMBER 11, 2001

CANADA

American Airlines
flight 11

Boston

United Airlines
flight 175

United Airlines
flight 93

New York City

Shanksville

U S A

Washington, D.C.

ATLANTIC
OCEAN

American Airlines
flight 77

Note: Dashed line indicates
speculative flight path because
the plane's transponder was
turned off during the hijacking.

These are the routes of the four ill-fated airliners that were hijacked on 11 September 2001.

ultra-fundamentalist policies, which included the exclusion of women from public life. The fact that they harboured al-Qaeda and refused to extradite Osama bin Laden after 9/11 meant that their days were now numbered.

'Enduring Freedom'

Although a manhunt was now on to get Osama bin Laden, it was part of a wider 'War on Terror' that

Islamic terrorists broke into the aircraft cockpits and took control of the planes.

involved initially an attack on the Taliban regime in Afghanistan. The United States had learned something from history and, instead of rolling in large conventional forces, it initially conducted a Special Forces insertion spearheaded by 5th Special Forces Group (Airborne), part of Joint Special Operations Task Force North, or Task Force Dagger. They were supported by 160th Special Operations Aviation Regiment. At about the same time, elements of the British SAS were also deployed into Afghanistan with the clear aim of finding Osama bin Laden and al-Qaeda.

To search for one individual in an area as large and as inaccessible as the mountains and passes of Afghanistan was never going to be easy. To make matters more complicated, a complex network of tunnels had been created, partly funded by the US CIA during the Soviet occupation, to allow anyone escape from one cave to another.

Tora Bora

Despite the immense geographical difficulties, Allied forces managed to narrow down the likely hiding place of Osama bin Laden to a region known as Tora Bora. Tora Bora is a network of caves located in eastern Afghanistan, near to the

Tora Bora

Tora Bora was a cave complex where it was thought Osama bin Laden was hiding. He is believed to have escaped while Allied forces attacked the complex.

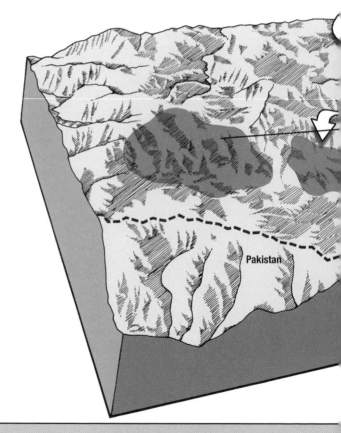

Pakistan

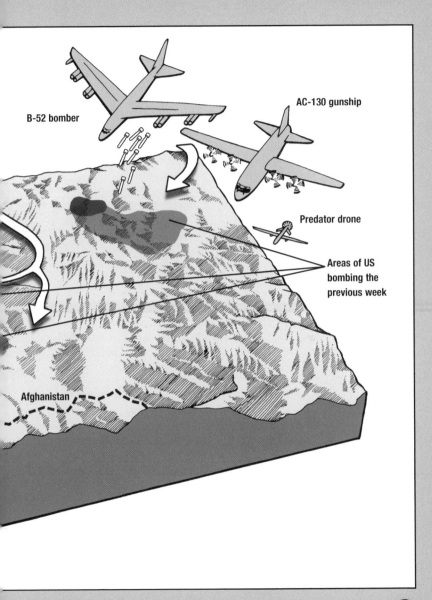

B-52 bomber

AC-130 gunship

Predator drone

Areas of US
bombing the
previous week

Afghanistan

Khyber Pass. Intelligence suggested that the network of caves here constituted a veritable underground city, which included living quarters with electric power as well as a vast cache of ammunition and missiles.

US and British Special Forces were both in the area, providing reconnaissance and guiding in air strikes, but there was also a ground combat element that included Afghan militia. This was a controversial part of the operation. As the al-Qaeda fighters retreated, and were clearly on the back foot, they negotiated a ceasefire with a local Afghan militia commander. Many believe that it was at this point that Osama bin Laden and his close companions managed to slip away from Tora Bora and towards the Pakistan border.

After Tora Bora, the manhunt continued. The intelligence operation was partly based on information gathered from the interrogation of al-Qaeda captives and on intercepts, such as a letter in late 2005 from a senior member of al-Qaeda to a commander of a camp for terrorist recruits, which moved bin Laden's possible locations from Waziristan to the Chitral District in northern Pakistan. What these regions had in common was that they were mountainous and controlled by unruly local warlords. Patrols that were sent there not surprisingly returned empty-handed.

Interrogation

One of the most controversial aspects of this information-gathering was interrogation, or rather the methods employed in the process of interrogation.

One of the al-Qaeda detainees said to have given up essential information under duress was Khalid Sheikh Mohammed. While he did not give full details of other al-Qaeda members, he did provide a list of nicknames, one of which was 'al-Kuwaiti'. In a manhunt a nickname is just a nickname until it pops up again in another context. When Hassan Ghul, another high-ranking member of al-Qaeda, was arrested in Iraq, he confirmed that 'al-Kuwaiti' was not only important but also closely associated with none other than al-Qaeda's director of operations, Abu Faraj al-Libi.

Ramzi bin al-Shibh

The post-9/11 manhunt was of course not focused exclusively on Osama bin Laden, although he remained the big catch. The US National Security Agency (NSA), based at Fort Meade in Maryland,

Profile of Osama bin Laden

Osama bin Laden was born in Riyadh, Saudi Arabia, probably on 10 March 1957, as part of a family of 50 children, the son of a self-made billionaire. His father, Mohammed bin Laden, was married 52 times, though he only had four wives at any one time. Osama received tuition as a Wahhabi Muslim and later became a member of the Muslim Brotherhood. Osama was extremely religious and was influenced by those who called for a *jihad*, or holy war, against the Soviet invasion of Afghanistan.

Osama bin Laden had been impressed by the Iranian Revolution, when a radical Islamist state was created in place of a westernized dictatorship. He was much less impressed, however, with the Saudi Arabian Government's response to the takeover of the mosque at Mecca by radicals. The Government only succeeded in regaining control with the help of French Special Forces. He was also unimpressed when the Saudi Government allowed US troops into the country in large numbers during the Persian Gulf War.

In 1998, bin Laden organized a series of bombings against US embassies in Nairobi, Kenya and Dar es Salaam, which killed 224 people; and in 2000, the destroyer USS *Cole* was the target of a suicide attack in the port of Aden, in which 17 US sailors were killed and 39 wounded.

These attacks proved to be a prelude to the massive attack on New York and Washington on 11 September 2001.

was given information that Ramzi bin al-Shibh was in the area, possibly along with Khalid Sheikh Mohammed. Ramzi bin al-Shibh had been central to the planning of the 9/11 attacks and acted as an intermediary.

Once the NSA received the tip-off, it concentrated massive electronic resources on the area, including a network of geosynchronous satellites. The fact that bin al-Shibh was unwise enough to use a satphone made things easier for the NSA. Not only did they have the ability to listen in to the calls, their SIGINT satellites were designed to move in orbit in such a way as to make it possible to pinpoint the geographical location of the satphone. The Pakistani Inter-Services Intelligence (ISI) Agency was alerted and on 11 September 2002, with the aid of the CIA's Special Activities Division, they intercepted bin al-Shibh and captured him after a gun battle.

The ability to intercept cell-phone calls also led US agents to Abu Faraj al-Libi. He was arrested by Pakistani Special Forces and the CIA Special Activities Division. Al-Libi was riding on the back of a motorcycle near Mardan in Pakistan when he was intercepted on 2 May 2005. When al-Libi was interrogated, he gave away

information that he had been promoted after the capture of Khalid and that he had received the message from a courier. As he was a very senior member of al-Qaeda, intelligence operatives construed that the courier must have brought a message straight from Osama bin Laden himself. In which case, identifying and following this courier would lead them to bin Laden.

Identifying the courier required a great deal of cross-referencing of intelligence material as well as new intelligence research, including material gathered from interrogations at the detention centre at Guantanamo Bay. By 2007, however, US intelligence had zeroed in on one man – Sheikh abu Ahmed, one of Osama bin Laden's most trusted lieutenants. Abu Ahmed has been close to Khalid and had been involved in the 9/11 attacks. A phone tap of another al-Qaeda operative provided a vital clue that they were on the right track. Intelligence operatives now knew the broad geographical location in which abu Ahmed was located. Once he had been identified, he was watched by ground surveillance agents and also tracked using high-technology assets such as drones and satellites, but would he lead them to the prize capture of bin Laden…

Timeline

1957: Osama bin Mohammad bin Awad bin Laden is born
in Riyadh, Saudi Arabia.

1988: Al-Qaeda – 'the Base' – established in Afghanistan
as a centre for radical Muslims joined in opposition to the
US, Israel and its allies.

1996: Bin Laden leaves Sudan for Afghanistan. He issues fatwa
against all US military personnel, which is faxed to supporters
across the world.

1998: Truck bomb explosions at US embassies in Kenya
and Tanzania, killing 224, including 12 Americans.
Bin Laden is added to FBI's '10 most wanted fugitives' list.

11 September 2001: 8.46 a.m. and 9.03 a.m.:
two planes crash into the north and south towers of the
World Trade Center. At 9.37 a.m. a third plane is crashed into
the Pentagon. At 10.03 a.m. a fourth crashes into a field.

7 October 2001: War in Afghanistan begins with US and UK
mounting bombing campaign.

12–17 December 2001: Battle of Tora Bora, where Osama bin
Laden is believed to be hiding.

September 2002: Al-Jazeera broadcasts poor-quality tape
claimed to be voice of Bin Laden, praising 9/11 hijackers
for changing 'the course of history'.

November 2002: Al-Qaida claims responsibility for three suicide
car bombs at the Mombasa Paradise resort hotel, killing 15
and wounding 80.

1 March 2003: Khalid Sheikh Mohammed is captured in
Rawalpindi, Pakistan, by Pakistani ISI.

2 May 2005: Abu Faraj al-Libi, third in command at al-Qaeda,
is arrested by the ISI and CIA Special Activities Division.

11 September 2002: Ramzi bin al-Shibh, a facilitator of 11
September attacks on New York and Washington, is arrested
in Karachi, Pakistan.

A manhunt involves the organized search for and tracking of a person, normally because that person has committed a crime and has afterwards disappeared. The manhunt normally involves various degrees of the skill of tracking, which extends from the skills used by primitive hunters to high-tech devices, including satellite reconnaissance. This book covers the various tools used in tracking and how they have been put to practical use in a range of high-profile manhunts, including the hunts for Saddam Hussein and Osama bin Laden.

Tracking and Stealth

Tracking, which is the central skill and science involved in a manhunt, has developed over millennia for very basic reasons. From prehistoric times, hunters used tracking skills to find both large and small game to eat. These skills would have involved a high level of intuitive understanding of types of animal track and other clues as to their whereabouts, and would have been taught to succeeding generations as the

. . . .

Manhunts involve skills that have been developed for thousands of years. Still used by native peoples for traditional hunting methods, they are also learned by Boy Scouts and military forces.

Hours of training and preparation go into making a successful military manhunt.

Introduction

Hunting

The skills used in a manhunt are often very similar to those used by hunters in search for game, such as the San people of southern Africa.

most basic and essential form of schooling. Successful tracking would ultimately lead to the killing of the animal for food and the end of the hunt.

Quite apart from the skill of reading signs on the ground and in the environment, which will be discussed in detail in this book, trackers also needed to learn the art of stealth. There would be no point successfully following a track and then scaring the animal away. The same principles are involved in a manhunt. The target has to be successfully tracked without them knowing that they are being followed or are close to capture. The final approach has to involve a large element of skill and surprise, otherwise the target may have time to get away. This book will cover final approach techniques that enable trackers to capture or kill their target before the target sees them.

Traditional Skills

Although many of the skills of tracking that are used in a manhunt date back millennia, many are still used by primitive peoples today, preserving a living memory of these fundamental skills. Such peoples include the aborigines of Australia, the San or Bushmen of southern Africa and the Native Americans of both North and South America.

The author Bruce Chatwin wrote in his book *Songlines* of the mysterious ancient pathways, invisible to the eyes of modern western man, that criss-crossed Australia. The paths were recognized by those Aborigines who had learned from their forefathers the art of recognizing plants, rocks and waterholes in their traditional hunting grounds, and were able to find their way where others, without a map and compass, would simply get lost and die.

The San of southern Africa, quite apart from their skill of tracking and stalking animals, also had an amazing ability to persevere in following large, fast animals at an easy trot, with which they covered huge distances, eventually wearing down their prey. This highlights another aspect of the manhunt – the ability to persevere. The hunt for Osama bin Laden, for example, took the best part of a decade. Another characteristic of the San was that they developed different types of poison to tip their arrows for different types of game.

Likewise, in a manhunt, the correct choice of weaponry needs to be selected for different targets. Although the San are famous for their marathon-like hunting trips, they were also skilled in building traps for animals to fall into. They even built a trap large enough to kill a hippopotamus by digging a hidden pit with a large wooden spike in it. In a manhunt, sometimes the best solution is to create a trap or ambush

Tracking

**Tracking is an essential skill for those who follow
game using traditional methods. Modern tracking
methods have been developed from these skills.**

for the target to walk into. The San would sometimes follow a predator, such as a lion, to a kill. In a similar way, intelligence units and Special Forces followed Osama bin Laden's courier to his hiding place.

European Manhunters

Whether in Africa, America, Australasia or elsewhere, the skills of tracking and hunting were soon learned by Europeans who settled in these areas and often they became as skilled as the natives. As the Europeans brought relatively sophisticated armaments with them, such as muskets, a new style of hunting was born. The US Rangers owe their name to groups of men who used to hunt down their enemies by ranging far afield. Colonel Benjamin Church (c. 1639–1718), who formed the first official ranger company, made a point of using Native American hunting techniques.

The British who fought against the Boers in southern Africa during the Boer Wars (1880–81 and 1899–1902) found themselves up against a formidable enemy who had learned many techniques from hunting that were also extremely useful in warfare. As the British began to pick up some of these techniques, some of them, like Robert Baden-Powell, began to beat the enemy at their own game. Baden-Powell's experiences in Africa inspired him to set up the Scouting

Bin Laden latest:

Sheikh abu Ahmed leads ground surveillance agents to a large house in an affluent suburb of Abbottabad.

movement, so that boys and young men learned, among many other outdoor skills, how to track and stalk game. His first experience of doing this was not in Africa but in the woods near Charterhouse School in Godalming, Surrey, when he was playing truant.

Baden-Powell developed many of his tracking and reconnaissance skills when he was serving in Africa among the Zulu tribes. He later met Frederick Russell Burnham, who had been a scout and tracker for the US Army in the Apache and Cheyenne wars. As the Wild West was tamed, Burnham transferred his skills to the British Army in Africa. Burnham was such a skilful tracker that the Africans called him 'He who sees in the dark'. Burnham was himself involved in a manhunt for the notorious chief Mlimo of the Matabele tribe, which was causing such trouble and which

Spearheads

The various spears seen here are used by hunters to finish off game that has been successfully tracked and followed using traditional methods.

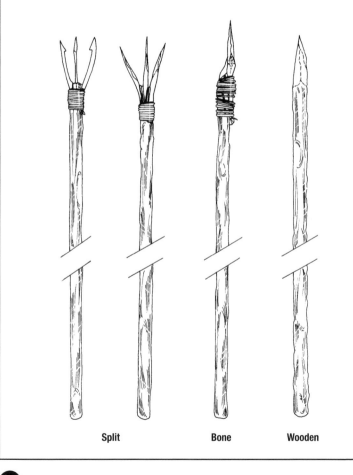

Split   Bone   Wooden

Scout Tracking

The Boy Scout movement was started on the basis of skills learned from Native Americans and other peoples who used traditional tracking methods.

Learning Stealth

Scouts learn the same stealth approach methods that native trackers and hunters and military forces also use.

had ambushed a British force. By using their tracking and stealth skills, Burnham and a companion made their way into a cave used by Mlimo and shot him dead.

Burnham was appointed as Chief of Scouts by the British commander Lord Roberts, which was an honour for a non-British officer. Burnham soon demonstrated his exceptional tracking skills as well as some of the skills still taught to Special Forces today. When he was captured by the Boers, for example, Burnham pretended to be wounded and was put among a group of loosely guarded wounded men. While being transported to a holding base, he slipped off the wagon of wounded men and lay motionless by the side of the road for four days before returning to the British lines. The principle of early escape is still taught to Special Forces today. Burnham later blew up a railway line, despite being severely wounded after a fall from a horse. He was awarded the Distinguished Service Order (DSO) by the British for his exploits.

When Burnham and Baden-Powell met during the Second Matabele War, they shared their mutual interest in scouting, reconnaissance and

tracking skills. Burnham taught Baden-Powell the skills of woodcraft he had learned on the North American frontier and Baden-Powell's acknowledgement of these skills was his choice of a Stetson-style hat and a kerchief, which also became emblematic of early scouting. Native tracking skills from both America and Africa were the underlying skills that civilized Europeans had re-learned from native peoples who still had an unbroken link with the traditional skills of the ancient past.

Another famous hunter of this period was Frederick Courteney Selous (1851–1917), who was a British explorer, hunter and army officer. Selous had been interested in natural history as a boy and spent as much time as possible outdoors. When he travelled to South Africa, Selous conducted scouting expeditions for Cecil Rhodes and also met Frederick Burnham and Robert Baden-Powell. Selous's long forays on hunting expeditions resulted in a host of adventures, including getting lost in the wilderness for days and close encounters with lions. The many adventures of Selous, and his influence on the area, inspired the

Selous Scouts

The Selous Scouts were formed in Rhodesia to conduct counter-insurgency operations, at which they became highly adept.

creation of the Selous Scouts, a Special Forces counter-insurgency unit that operated in Rhodesia between 1973 and 1980. This regiment had particular expertise in tracking.

The tracking skills of tribes handed down over millennia, the learning of these skills by high-profile and inspirational individuals such as Burnham, Baden-Powell and Selous, and the use of these skills by modern military forces provides a consistent story of tracking to the present day.

These skills have also been refined for the modern technological age, so that a modern manhunt retains the intuitive skills that a Native American, for example, would employ on his quest for food, complemented with sophisticated electronic tracking and a range of other intelligence.

Insignia

The osprey, a large bird of prey, was the symbol of the Selous Scouts Special Forces regiment.

The forces and technology involved in a modern manhunt cover a very broad range across all fighting services and across a myriad of skills and technology. As mentioned in the Introduction, a manhunt may involve ancient hunting skills and high-tech satellite surveillance. There is not room in this chapter to cover every detail in this broad spectrum of training but it is worth looking at some of the relevant training skills for particular units, such as Special Forces units and intelligence operatives.

Special Forces and aircrew receive particularly focused training in escape and evasion and survival for the reason that they are most likely to find themselves cut off from regular logistical supplies and other military support and also have a higher likelihood of capture. Although advanced technology and systems such as GPS often mean that downed aircrew may call in rescue missions to extract them from enemy territory, they are also taught to survive and find their way back to safety if this should not be possible. Special Forces involved in advanced

· ·

Elite soldiers undertake rigorous training in order to survive and to evade enemy forces. They are also taught invaluable tracking and counter-tracking skills and covert movement.

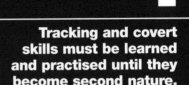

1

Tracking and covert skills must be learned and practised until they become second nature.

Training

reconnaissance who may find themselves behind enemy lines are taught the same skills. In the British armed forces these forces include the Special Air Service (SAS), Special Boat Squadron and Special Forces Signals. In the United States, similar units would include 1st Special Forces Operational Detachment-Delta, the US Navy Special Warfare Development Group, including Navy SEALs, and US Air Force 24th Special Tactics Squadron. Associated elite forces include the British Parachute Regiment, Pathfinders and Royal Marines and the US 75th Ranger Regiment and the US Marine Corps Force Reconnaissance.

Special Forces Training

Various different Special Forces and elite units from various countries will have their own characteristic way of training for escape and evasion but certain principles will apply across the range. The soldiers will be taught how to survive off the land. This training will typically involve soldiers being taken to a remote area where they will be deprived of their usual food supplies. To start things off and use up any reserves from their last major meal, they may be sent on a tough march over an area such as the Brecon Beacons, where the British SAS and other Special Forces regularly train. This sort of route march would be tiring enough even with regular supplies of food and water. Exhausted from the trek and with night setting in, they will have to build their own campsite in a covert area, using nothing other than the equipment they have available in their 'escape kit'. This bag of tricks is effectively their only means of survival. Soldiers will have undergone

Using GPS

The Global Positioning System provides instant positional awareness. This makes it a useful tool when conducting a manhunt.

a thorough check to ensure that they do not carry any large pieces of extra equipment or food supplies to make things easier.

They will then have to make camp and forage for food, bearing in mind a high level of physical fatigue and also that they will have limited equipment to keep rain off and cold out, and no such comforts as a sleeping bag. The best they can hope for is a heat-shield survival blanket which will provide minimal comfort. They will need to light a fire if they can with their escape kit equipment and cook whatever can be foraged, if anything.

Typical Contents of an Escape Kit

A soldier should carry an escape kit somewhere on his person (i.e. on his personal webbing vest or in a pocket) and not in a large bergen, which might have to be left behind in a hurry. What is sometimes known as a 'belt kit' may include other essential items, such as a light packable waterproof and some food. In an emergency, Special Forces soldiers are taught to drop their heavy bergens if there is no alternative.

The minimum survival tools in an escape kit may include:

Equipment for fire lighting
- Matches
- Candles (sometimes these are edible)
- Flint and steel

Signalling equipment
- A mirror or alternatively the inside of the survival tin itself
- A flare may be carried separately

Water purification equipment
- Water purification tablets
- Water filtration bag

Equipment to catch food
- Animal snares
- Fishing line and hooks

In addition, it is advisable to carry either a Swiss Army knife or Leatherman-style tool ,as these will prove invaluable for a range of uses from cutting branches for shelter to preparing food. On training exercises, however, such equipment is not always allowed.

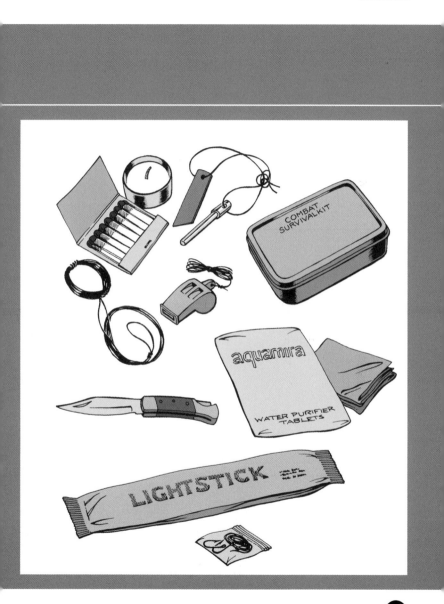

Universal Edibility Test

Food is obviously a vital part of survival and it is not always possible to identify plants accurately or those that are edible and those that are not. The Universal Edibility Test is designed to plot a careful course through experimenting with plants that might be edible.

1. Test only one part of a potential food plant at a time.

2. Separate the plant into its basic components – leaves, stems, roots, buds and flowers.

3. Smell the food to see if you can detect any strong acid odours. Smell is not enough of a test for whether a plant is edible or not.

4. Fast for eight hours before starting the test.

5. Test the plant for contact poisoning by placing it under your arm or on the inside of your elbow or wrist.

6. During the test period, drink only water and eat only the plant in question.

7. Take a small part of the plant and initially touch it to your lip to test for irritation.

8. If there is no irritation, place the sample on your tongue and leave it there for 15 minutes.

9. If there are no undue side effects, you can swallow the food.

10. If there are bad side effects, make yourself vomit the food and then drink plenty of water.

11. Assuming all is well, continue to eat more of the plant.

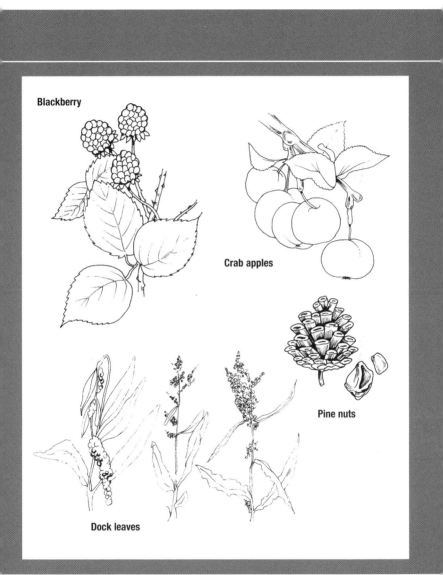

Blackberry

Crab apples

Pine nuts

Dock leaves

Nettle Tea

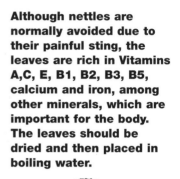

Although nettles are normally avoided due to their painful sting, the leaves are rich in Vitamins A,C, E, B1, B2, B3, B5, calcium and iron, among other minerals, which are important for the body. The leaves should be dried and then placed in boiling water.

Scott O'Grady

On 2 June 1995, US Air Force captain Scott O'Grady was patrolling in an F-16 jet fighter over the former Yugoslavia when he was hit by a surface-to-air missile near Banja Luka. O'Grady safely ejected but found himself facing a second problem – how to keep out of sight in enemy territory until he was picked up by friendly forces.

O'Grady managed to survive for six days by keeping himself well camouflaged and moving as little as possible while Serbian forces searched for him. His main concern was finding enough water to drink. Although he had some water in his emergency kit, he also had to collect rainwater to avoid dehydration.

O'Grady was carrying a signal beacon and a daring rescue was organized by the 24th Marine Expeditionary Unit (Special Operations Capable) aboard USS *Kearsarge*. The rescue helicopter identified O'Grady's location and he put out a flare at the last moment to guide them in. Once he had been picked up, the helicopters came under attack from surface-to-air missiles and small-arms fire but managed to get away.

This incident showed how a modern escape can involve basic survival skills as well as modern technology.

The following day will typically consist of demonstrations on how to slaughter and cook animals, whether it be sheep or rabbits, and make such delicacies as nettle tea.

Unpalatable as these may be, the students will do well to eat as much as they can for they will soon be off on another route march to test their navigation skills.

The US Marine Corps mixes reconnaissance skills with sniper skills, the understandable logic being that a sniper has to learn the skills to get in sight of the enemy without being seen and therefore get into a position to provide key intelligence on enemy movements.

The US Marine Corps can also call on the services of the Forces Reconnaissance Companies (Force Recon), which now fall under Marine Special Operations Command. These units typically assess beach landing sites prior to assault by main units, providing information on suitability

Finding Water

Water is the essential means of survival, even before food. In fact, if water is scarce, you should take care not to eat too much food, especially bulky food that needs lots of water to break it down.

- It helps to have an idea where water is most likely to be found.

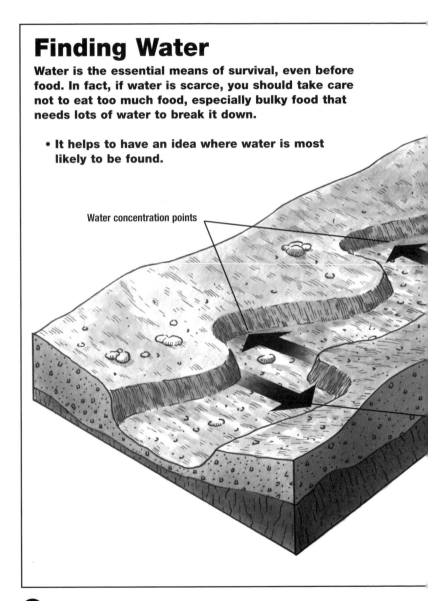

Water concentration points

Water concentration points

- In dry valleys, gulleys and watercourses, water will usually collect at the lowest point, on the outside of a bend.
- Animals, birds and insects may be heading in the direction of water, or coming from it. Follow their paths, if necessary by tracking their footprints or other kinds of spoor.
- Any sign of greenery will indicate the presence of water.
- At the foot of cliffs or rock outcrops, water may collect in holes and fissures.
- Sometimes water may be seen trickling out from a crack in a rock and may be a sign of a larger supply. If necessary, the water might be accessed by creating a straw to suck it from grass.
- Water holes are sometimes identifiable due to the mounds of animal excrement around them.

Sniper Training

Snipers are taught many of the skills that are required in successful tracking and covert movement. They can remain hidden for long periods and move unseen within range of their target.

The ultimate aim of a manhunt is making contact with the target. This may mean creating the conditions for capture or eliminating a target who is armed and dangerous.

of the ground as well as enemy movements.

Among British Special Forces, of particular relevance to manhunt operations is the relatively newly formed Special Reconnaissance Regiment. This regiment was established in 2005 as a new component of United Kingdom Special Forces (UKSF), incorporating also the Special Air Service (SAS), Special Boat Service (SBS) and Special Forces Support Group (SFSG). The brief for the new regiment was largely covert special reconnaissance and surveillance. A unit of this type would be closely involved in providing essential surveillance information during the course of a manhunt. Training

for the Special Reconnaissance Regiment is rigorous and is understood to involve a range of relevant skills such as photography, surveillance, reconnaissance and advanced driving, along with close-quarter battle (CQB) skills. Candidates would also be put through combat survival and resistance to interrogation (RTI) training.

The SAS

Training for different units varies according to factors such as their native environment, their role and so on. Before training begins, however, a process of rigorous selection must take place.

For the British SAS, this selection process takes place largely in the Brecon Beacons in Wales. The

Ambush Training

Ambush training works two ways. First, it provides experience for soldiers who are learning how to deal with capture and interrogation. Second, it trains the soldiers who are conducting the ambush to stop a moving vehicle and take the occupants captive.

Selection Training

Elite and special forces are put through rigorous selection training in challenging outdoor environments. The selection is designed to ensure that the soldiers will be able to endure the challenges of covert military operations.

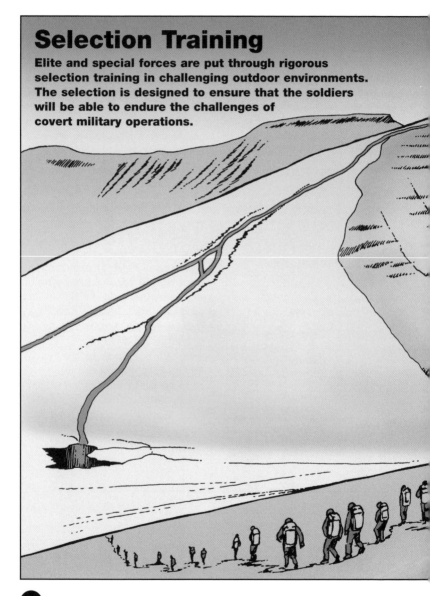

highest mountain in the Brecon Beacons is Pen y Fan at 886m (2906ft). Selection for the SAS lasts for a month and it is assumed that candidates are fit before they arrive. As the SAS demands supreme fitness, the candidates have time to build up their fitness during the first week. The candidates are then sent on long forced marches over the Brecon Beacons and the Black Mountains. The particular topography of the Brecons makes for very demanding walking terrain, with false summits appearing all the time, each one revealing that the candidate has further to go.

The weight of the bergen is gradually increased as the days and weeks go on, and the candidates have to prove that they can navigate successfully through the rugged landscape and perform a range of other tasks when cold, wet and tired. Getting navigation wrong on the Brecon Beacons can be fatal, as it is easy to fall down steep slopes in the dark or in stormy weather. Another danger is exposure and hypothermia in the bleak windswept hills.

Counter-tracking procedures are built into SAS training even at this stage because when the candidates are given instructions, they are not allowed to write anything down or even mark their maps. This would prevent an enemy from gaining any information if any of them were captured. As time goes on, even maps become a luxury and they have little to go on other than rudimentary sketch maps.

Once the gruelling selection in the Brecon Beacons is over, the successful candidates will move on to the six-month Continuation course, where they will learn how to operate behind enemy lines, signalling and a range of specialist skills, including sniping, how to bring in aerial and artillery fire, survival skills, sabotage and demolition, and handling a range

Insignia

The Special Reconnaissance Regiment is the newest British Special Forces unit.

Jungle Training

Jungle training provides the ultimate in covert movement. Due to the depth of foliage, an enemy may only be metres away and remain unseen.

Bravo Two Zero

The exploits of the SAS unit Bravo Two Zero demonstrate some aspects of escape and evasion, the underlying one being that nothing beats training and sheer determination. The SAS and other Special Forces recruit people carefully to ensure that they have the right qualities – and Chris Ryan proved they were right.

In January 1991, B Squadron 22 SAS were tasked with observing and reporting on the 'Scud' missiles that had been deployed into the Iraqi desert on mobile launchers to provide the regime of Saddam Hussein with a military and political tool to use against countries such as Israel. In order to prevent the Israelis retaliating in self-defence, it was important for the allies to neutralize the Scud threat. The desert was therefore divided into zones shared between the British SAS and United States Delta Force.

Despite the high standards maintained by British Special Forces and associated assets, things began to go wrong when the Bravo Two Zero troops were dropped by helicopter in a desert as hard as rock, with no available cover. Although temporarily they had the cover of night, they knew they would be horribly exposed the next morning to patrolling Iraqis, as they were only a few hundred yards from an Iraqi anti-aircraft battery. There was also a bitingly cold wind sweeping across the desert with no cover to mitigate it. There proved to be a problem with radio communications, so they could not order in a rescue flight to take them somewhere they could get on with their covert mission.

As dawn came, they were seen by a shepherd boy, who raised the alarm. It was not long before a truckload of Iraqi soldiers arrived and the SAS troopers attempted to run out of trouble, still carrying their heavy bergens with all their equipment, while keeping the Iraqis at bay with occasional rifle fire. As they were extremely overloaded with equipment, they had no choice but to ditch the bergens, which meant they had to face the desert and the extreme cold with minimal equipment. Of the eight members of the patrol, only one was to get away – Sergeant Chris Ryan. The others were either captured, shot and killed or died of hypothermia.

Ryan was now on his own, pacing across an open desert, either baked by sun during the day or lashed with freezing winds at night. He had to call on every ounce of his endurance training for the SAS. There was little or no cover and in due course a couple of Iraqi vehicles appeared out of the horizon behind him. Even an SAS trooper cannot outrun a vehicle. However, Ryan had managed to retain a disposable LAW 66mm (2.6in) US hand-held anti-tank weapon. Although the Iraqis might have felt the game was up, since there was only one man against two vehicles full of soldiers, unfortunately for them they were up against a soldier from the world's premier Special Forces regiment. According to his account, Ryan aimed his LAW at one vehicle and blew it up. He then reached for his M203 grenade launcher and destroyed the other. He finished off any surviving Iraqis with his M16 assault rifle. Leaving the burning wreckage in the desert, he resumed his extraordinary forced march. Ryan endured further days and nights of extreme temperature in the desert but kept going, despite inadequate food and water. Eventually he reached Syria and relative safety and was picked up by friendly forces.

This incident reveals what can happen when things go wrong and how even the most highly trained soldiers can be compromised. The wrong drop location, breakdowns in radio communications and the failure of a regular helicopter pick up at an agreed point due to pilot illness all contributed to the fiasco. In the stress of the moment, the soldiers were forced to drop valuable equipment, leaving behind some warm clothing that might have made the difference between survival and death or capture. It has been noted that the man who got away, Chris Ryan, was the only one who wore non-army issue boots. He had spent his own money on a high-quality and expensive boot that provided maximum comfort during his forced march.

The point of continuous training is to ensure that, in circumstances such as these, when there is no time to think, the soldiers are fully prepared both in knowing what to do and in carrying the right equipment for an emergency.

Endurance Techniques

However fit you are and however well trained, there is a limit to how long you can realistically expect to survive in hot desert conditions if you have limited water supplies. With about a litre of water, resting during the day and

walking at night, you should last about two and a half days. Sergeant Chris Ryan survived the harsh conditions because of his endurance training for the SAS.

of unusual weapons. They will learn to forget many of the routines they will have learned in the regular army, such as platoon drills and the spit and polish of those days. They will now operate in a four-man team where everyone is more or less equal according to their specialism, and where uniform is what is required by the environment and circumstances. Here the SAS reflects the inspiration of one of their spiritual founders, T.E. Lawrence, who wrote in *Seven Pillars of Wisdom*: 'The efficiency of our forces was the professional efficiency of the single man   Our ideal should be to make our battle a series of single combats, our ranks a happy alliance of agile commanders-in-chief.'

A vital aspect of ongoing SAS training is the ability to survive behind enemy lines without support and it is during this phase that they learn escape and evasion, tracking and counter-tracking, building shelters and foraging for food and so on. At some point, they will be deliberately set up for capture by their instructors so that they can go through the process of resistance to interrogation (RTI). A typical scenario may be the ambush of a lorry in which the recruits are being transported by a friendly agent. They will probably be ambushed by regular soldiers, for whom this also provides essential training. They will be taken out under gunpoint, with sandbags placed over

their heads and their hands bound behind their back. They will be transported to an interrogation centre, where they may face a long period facing a wall with no contact with their colleagues until eventually they are taken into an interrogation room, where they will then be subjected to a range of interrogation techniques. Again, this provides training for the interrogators as much as for the soldiers. The underlying training concept is to remain a 'grey' man and to provide as little information as possible, other than name, rank and number.

The SAS recruits then go on to a jungle survival centre, in Brunei or some other destination in the Far East. They are trained in the full range of jungle survival, navigation and movement. After this, recruits train in their various chosen specialisms, which might be Boat, Air, Mountain or Mobility Troop.

US Navy SEALs

Some of the toughest training for any Special Forces in the world is undertaken by the US Navy SEALs. Selection and training lasts at least a year, after which successful graduates are awarded the Special Warfare Operator Naval Rating and Navy Enlisted Classification (NEC) 5326 Combatant Swimmer (SEAL). Officers are awarded the designation Naval Special Warfare (SEAL) Officer. After volunteering from either the US

Drown Proofing

Recruits for the US Navy Seals have to pass severe tests in water survival with their hands and feet tied. They must bob for five minutes, float for five minutes, swim 100m (328ft) and bob for two minutes, do forward and back flips, swim to the bottom of the pool to retrieve an object with their teeth, then bob five times.

Hell Week

Hell Week is Week 4 of Phase One training for US Navy SEAL recruits. For five and a half days, the recruits endure a series of gruelling tasks, including lying in the cold surf as it washes over their heads and bodies, and carrying heavy objects with telegraph posts.

Navy or Coastguard, candidates must pass an initial screening test that includes swimming, push-ups, sit-ups, pull-ups and a run.

First, the applicants attend a course at Naval Special Warfare Preparation School and, if they pass through this, they move on to a 25-week Basic Underwater Demolition/SEAL (BUD/S) training course at the Naval Special Warfare Center at Naval Amphibious Base Coronado, California. Here, the intensely physically demanding regime continues. The apex of the training regime is a 132-hour period of almost continual physical activity known as 'Hell Week' where the recruits are constantly cold, wet or covered in mud or sand. The real test in Hell Week is the mental endurance that pushes through the physical pain. One of the most formidable obstacles is cold. Recruits lie on a beach as the ice-cold surf rolls over them and they never seem to be able to get warm and dry. On top of this, they do not sleep for more than four hours. Candidates drop out for a variety of reasons: some because they simply cannot take it; and some because they suffer physical injuries or succumb to the cold. Only about 25 per cent of candidates make it through this stage. Ultimately, it is a question of who wants it most. Part of the endurance depends on teamwork – buddies pull each other through and stop each other falling asleep. This mutual dependence is what they will

Bin Laden latest:

The house in Abbottabad is put under close surveillance, using sophisticated electronic assets as well as agents on the ground.

need on operations, when up against a ruthless enemy or when wounded. They will be able to achieve what regular service personnel might consider impossible.

After graduation from BUD/S, successful candidates go on to SEAL Qualification Training (SQT), a 26-week course designed to teach a range of skills that a fully qualified SEAL will require in order to be operational. The range of courses include Tactical Air Operations (static line/freefall), Tactical Combat Medicine, Communications, Advanced Special Operations, Cold Weather/Mountaineering, Maritime Operations, Combat Swimmer, Tactical Ground Mobility, Land Warfare (small unit tactics, light and heavy weapons, demolitions), armed (CQ) and unarmed combat (MMA/USA/USMC style), Close

Tracking an Injured Person

Trackers can gather information from the appearance of tracks, including whether a person is injured or not. A person who has an injured leg, for example, is likely to tread more lightly on that side and perhaps place the forward part of the foot on the ground. The other imprint will be more defined.

Bootprints

A tracker will be able to identify a target from the pattern of their shoe or boot. To distinguish between soldiers with the same-issue boots, the tracker will look for particular aspects of wear in the tread that identify an individual.

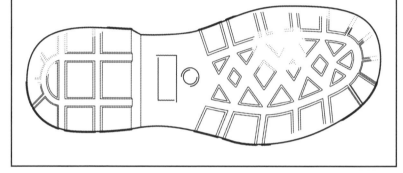

Combat Weapons and Assaults/ Close Quarters Combat.

Once SQT is completed, recruits are awarded the Navy NEC 5326, the Navy SEAL Trident, and are assigned to a SEAL Team.

Tracking

As this book is primarily about the skills used in a manhunt, the full range of Special Forces training will not be discussed in detail. However, as part of training for escape and evasion, tracking and counter-tracking is relevant, as there is a high likelihood that Special Forces soldiers will be subjected to tracking when moving out of an area of operations.

Special Forces training for escape and evasion involves elements such as: survival training; covert movement (despite being highly effective soldiers in combat, success in these circumstances depends on not engaging with the enemy); camouflage techniques; navigation techniques (these will include navigation without formal aids such as a map and compass); and, ultimately, signalling and recovery techniques.

The Special Forces soldier's awareness of tracking and his vulnerability to being tracked and captured will result in extreme caution when moving on the ground.

The most obvious track that a hostile tracker can use is a footprint, which is also known as a 'spoor'. Experienced trackers can identify one given individual in a group by the particular characteristics of a footprint. In his famous book *Scouting for Boys,* Robert Baden-Powell uses an example of an old-fashioned hobnail boot, as were once issued to soldiers, and how a particular boot could be identified, if one or more of the nails were missing, for example. A modern boot will have a particular tread pattern according to the make (it may or may not be regular army issue) or have identifiable wear patterns. Even a stone caught in the tread of a boot may leave a significant imprint on the ground.

The tracker can glean other clues from the footprints, such as their spacing and the depth of impression on the ground. For example, an uneven impression between right and left footprints may indicate that the target is favouring one leg and is therefore wounded. These clues and characteristics will be discussed in more detail in a later chapter.

When training, military trackers are taught to keep any signs of track or spoor free from any interference. This is one of the most basic rules of tracking and one that is often forgotten. A report is then made on the basis of the information that can be gathered from the track or

Covering your Tracks

Covering your tracks may be possible in some circumstances but there is a danger that the attempt to cover them will be noticed by a good tracker and will only hold them up momentarily.

Double Tracking

A variety of methods can be used to try to shake off a tracker. Walking backwards is a common ruse but an experienced tracker will notice the sign of a deep heel imprint revealing what the target has been doing.

tracks, such as the number of people present, the direction of travel and the age of the track. An expert tracking team is then called in and the tracker will attempt to move as quickly as possible in the circumstances by looking at the tracks ahead of him and by making useful deductions. If the tracking is taking place in a hostile environment, the tracker will be protected by armed members of a patrol, the reason being that a tracker who is concentrating carefully on the evidence is quite vulnerable to attack. In hostile territory, signalling between trackers and members of the patrol will be done by hand.

Anyone who has watched the film *Butch Cassidy and the Sundance Kid* may remember that, when they are being trailed, they attempt to split their pursuers by sending a riderless horse in one direction while they ride pillion together on the other horse in another direction. For a while, the trackers are split but they are not fooled for long and return to the point at which the riders split. One can only guess what would have caused the trackers to become aware of the ruse. Perhaps a real tracker would have noticed the lighter indentation of the hooves of the riderless horse versus the heavier indentation of the horse that now had two riders. Whatever the reason, the trackers return to the point of the split and

Confusing the Tracker

Walking backwards out of a river is another ruse that can be used to confuse a tracker. Like many of the deception tactics, it will probably only slow down an experienced tracker for a short time as they work out what has happened.

follow the correct trail. Military trackers are taught to mark the point carefully at which the tracks split so that they can return to it if they have been led on a false trail. They are also taught to be aware of signs of a deception, such as an exaggerated track or disturbance on the ground and in surrounding vegetation. An experienced tracker will quickly recognize an attempt at deception. Likewise, if the track is not lost altogether, trackers are taught to mark the point where the track was last seen and then make a careful circular reconnaissance around the area to endeavour to pick up the track again.

Counter-Tracking

When counter-tracking, the soldier has constantly to be aware of ways in which he might be able to fool a pursuing tracker. One of these ways is to try to counter the tracker's intuition. If the track is faint and there is a choice of direction, which one would the tracker expect you to take? If there is a likely expectation, take the alternative. The soldier will be taught to avoid acting in a routine or regular way. It may be possible, for example, to lead a false trail and then remove any footwear before backtracking onto the original track. Alternatively, fit horse shoes or pieces of tyre rubber to the feet that might confuse a tracker. Another method is to walk on the sides of the feet.

It can be an advantage to move when it is raining, as heavy rain will wash away tracks and reduce the signature. Dull weather conditions also make it more difficult for a tracker to see the tracks. Counter-tracking techniques may include walking on hard ground wherever possible, walking backwards, stepping into existing footprints or walking in water. Such measures will only temporarily confuse an expert tracker and will have no effect at all against a tracker dog. The soldier will be aware of other clues that trackers can use, such as broken branches and material left behind from clothing snagged in branches or on rocks.

Another method of losing a pursuer is to confuse them by adopting a complex double-tracking system. One example of this is to walk towards a tree in a clearing for about five paces, then turn round and walk backwards and change direction by 90 degrees. The soldier can repeat this tactic of change of direction some distance further on. When approaching a trail, the soldier changes direction so as to approach at an angle of 45 degrees. Once he meets the trail, he breaks all the rules and leaves plenty of evidence for a tracker, including obvious footprints. He then retraces his steps backwards to the point where he joined the trail and then crosses over the trail, taking great care to not leave any trace of

Escape Maps and Compasses

Escape maps have become a familiar aspect of escape and evasion and part of the lore of secret operations, extending back to World War II.

During World War II, Christopher Clayton-Hutton was tasked with producing a map that could be carried clandestinely by British servicemen, particularly pilots, so that they would have a chance of getting back to safety once their aircraft had crashed. Hutton worked closely with the famous mapmakers Bartholomew, who allowed their maps to be used copyright free. Waddington PLC also became involved in the printing of maps, which were printed on either silk or a special thin tissue paper, which, instead of being made from conventional paper pulp but a special pulp created from crushed mulberry leaves, would be liable to degrade quickly, especially if wet. For both the silk and paper versions, it took some time to create the right kind of ink that would not fade or run in rigorous conditions. In addition to the maps, servicemen were also provided with tiny compasses that could be hidden in either buttons or in pens.

Modern US forces are also issued with Evasion Charts (EVC), based on the Joint Operations Graphic (JOG), which consists of 1:250,000-scale JOG charts. The alternative is a Tactical Pilotage Chart (1:500,000 scale). The maps are printed on strong, flexible material that is both waterproof and tear resistant. The EVC maps not only have a map that is relevant to the particular area but which also includes a range of other useful information for survival, including guidance on navigation techniques, survival medicine, environmental hazards and water and food procurement. There are also images of both edible and poisonous plants. The EVC maps and information are not designed to make up for lack of training. Successful escape and evasion for Special Forces will depend largely on thorough training and experience. However, they do provide essential information that complements rigorous training.

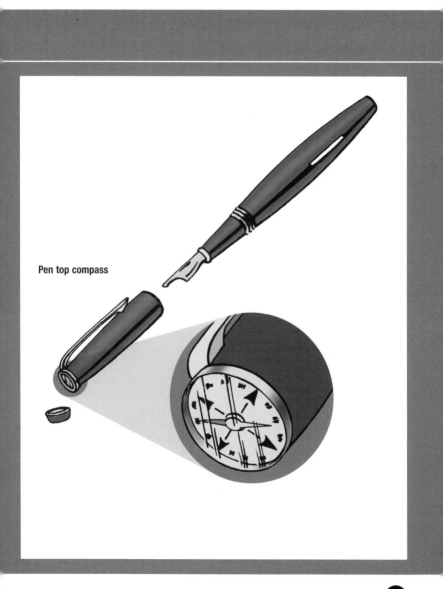

Pen top compass

his presence. Having crossed the trail, the soldier once again takes an angle of about 45 degrees and carries on for about 100m (328ft) and in reverse of his original line of advance.

If the soldier should reach a stream or shallow river, he moves into the water and walks along it for 100–200m (328–656ft). He stays as far as possible in the centre of the stream, if it is safe, where the water is deepest. At an appropriate point, he leaves the water, taking care not to leave any marks on vegetation or break twigs or branches. As an extra precaution, he leaves the water backwards so that it looks like an entry point if any footprints are spotted.

Escape

As part of their training, Special Forces will be taught the importance of early escape. This has been mentioned in the previous chapter using the example of Frederick Russell Burnham, who was quick to feign an injury once he had been captured by the Boers when he was fighting for the British in South Africa. Instinctively, and calling on experience from the American Indian frontier, Burnham knew that prisoners on the move had the best chance of escape and that those prisoners who were wounded would be less heavily guarded. He therefore feigned an injury and slipped off the wagon of wounded men at an opportune moment.

Likewise, soldiers are trained to look for opportunities and distractions whereby they can get away and make their escape. At this point, it is also difficult for the captors to send out a search party, as it may hold up their march and they also need to watch other prisoners.

There are a variety of other reasons why an early escape is likely to be the most successful.

- Enemy forces may still be relatively tired and disorganized after an engagement with opposing forces.
- They may have limited troops to assign to guarding prisoners.
- They may not know the area well and therefore find it difficult to follow and locate an escaped prisoner.
- There may still be the chance of an attack by friendly forces, which may provide enough distraction for an escape to be attempted.
- Once the enemy have reached their base, the chances of escape are reduced due to the fact that the prisoner may be placed in a cell or compound, and there will be full-time guards allocated to security.

Sometimes prisoners may be able to get together to plan an escape between them. One prisoner may feign an injury, such as a twisted ankle, or pretend to have a fit, or

US Army Field Manual Escape and Evasion

Every alternative should be considered before determining a course of action. For example:

- Travel restrictions such as curfews, checkpoints, and roadblocks will have to be anticipated.

- Local customs should be studied for possible imitation to avoid being conspicuous.

- Information on specific border areas should be obtained and studied.

The person who has been isolated in enemy-controlled territory needs to decide what equipment to keep and how and where to dispose of the remainder. The individual should presume that the descent or isolation has been observed by the enemy. The important thing is to avoid capture, even if it means leaving the scene of isolation and deviating from the evasion plan of action (EPA) or leaving valuable equipment behind.

may indeed be injured and collapse and refuse to go further. In these circumstances, when the guards are distracted, another prisoner may take the opportunity to get away.

If a prisoner does manage to slip away, he can adopt the counter-tracking techniques described earlier. His main priority will be to put as much distance between himself and his captors as possible

as it will be unlikely that they will want to leave their route of march for long.

Once a prisoner is in a compound, escape may prove more difficult, especially if it is closely guarded. Given time, the prisoner may have the opportunity to disguise himself and get out of the main entrance or make an attempt to climb over a fence under cover of night. To get

Make a Break for Freedom

Soldiers are taught to take the earliest opportunity to escape when captured. A distraction, such as an attack by friendly forces, may provide the ideal opportunity to make a break for freedom.

Climbing over a Fence

A barbed-wire fence can be a formidable obstacle. One method of getting over is to place a blanket or coat over the barbed wire. This can be an effective way of getting away from a pursuing tracker with a dog.

over a barbed-wire fence, it may be possible to place a blanket over the top of the fence and then roll over it. Escape methods will obviously depend on the particular circumstances of the camp. Sometimes prisoners manage to get away because they have closely monitored the movements of camp guards and know the right moment to take their opportunity.

Evasion

Evasion can sometimes take a long time, such as several weeks, or it may be a question of only a few hours. Once the prisoner has tasted freedom, he wants to make absolutely sure he is not recaptured and so training for Special Forces and aircrew focuses on a number of key areas.

Navigation

Obviously, the newly escaped soldier does not want to be running around in circles, and if he has been captured he will probably have lost his map and compass.

There are certain basic principles about the sun and stars that an evader can rely on for orientation. The sun rises in the east and sets in the west. At midday in the Northern Hemisphere, the sun is due south and due north in the Southern Hemisphere. If the evader has a watch, by holding it with the hour hand pointing to the sun, and imagining a line passing through

the 12, true south is between the hour hand and the 12. In the Southern Hemisphere, if the imaginary line through the 12 is pointed at the sun, then true north will be the midpoint between the 12 and the hour hand.

As it may be unlikely that an evader will still have his watch, another method of telling direction is to use shadow. Place a stick in the ground in a clear area where the shadow it casts can clearly be seen. Mark the shadow with a twig or a stone and wait for between 10 and 15 minutes while the shadow moves a few inches. Then mark the second position of the shadow. When you draw a line between the two marks, you will have an approximate east–west line. If the evader now stands with the first mark to the left and the second mark to the right, he is now facing north.

Another method is to place a stick about 50cm (2ft) high in a clear area of flat ground. Attach a piece of string to the stick and in the morning draw an arc around the base of the stick at the same radius as the shadow cast by the stick. Allow time to pass until the afternoon and when the shadow touches the arc again, make a second mark. The line between the two marked points is an east–west line. When this line is bisected, it forms a north–south line.

The stars can also be used to determine direction. In the Northern

Watch Navigation

A watch can be used to find north and south by pointing the hour hand at the sun and imagining a line passing through the 12. True south will be between the hour hand and the 12 in the southern hemisphere and true north in the northern hemisphere.

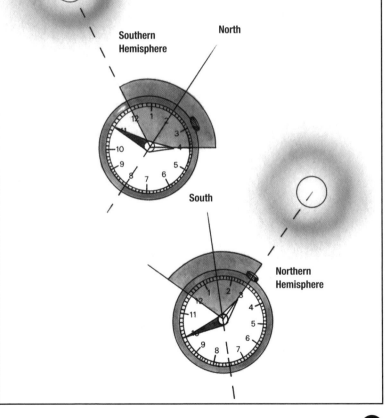

Southern Hemisphere

North

South

Northern Hemisphere

Pole Star

For centuries, navigators have used the North Star or Polaris as a guide. To check you are looking at the right star, follow the Plough and Cassiopea.

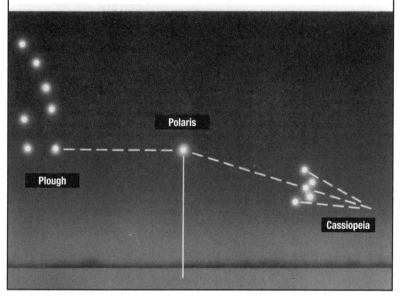

Hemisphere, the North Star, Polaris, is identified by following an imaginary line through the constellations of the Plough, Cassiopeia and Orion. In the Southern Hemisphere, you can multiply the longest axis of the Southern Cross by 4.5, which should bring you to an imaginary point above the horizon. Your southern landmark is directly beneath this point.

The movement of the stars can also be used to judge compass bearings.

First mark two points on the ground against which you can judge the movement of a star. If, while looking at the star, it appears to rise, you are looking approximately due east. If the star appears to descend, you are looking approximately due west. If it appears to move to the right, you are looking approximately due south, and if it appears to move to the left, then you are looking approximately due north.

Navigating by the Southern Cross

The most distinctive constellation in the Southern Hemisphere is the Southern Cross, which is accompanied by two bright 'trailing stars to its east (left).

The coalsack, a dark nebula, forms a starless area immediately southeast of the Southern Cross

When the Southern Cross appears upright in the night sky, a line dropped vertically down to the horizon beneath it indicates geographic south.

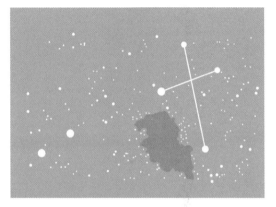

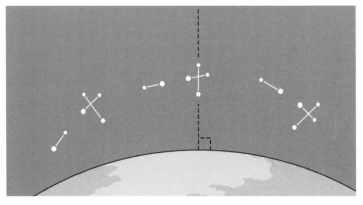

Time and Direction by Shadow

Evaders have successfully used this method of telling time and direction. As described in the text, the method is simple to remember and requires only a few sticks and the sun in order to work out both direction and time.

Fire

Lighting a fire can be dangerous if there is any chance that an enemy might see it. However, fire is also essential for warmth and cooking, and in the right circumstances it may be appropriate to attempt to light one. A survival kit will often contain windproof matches but these may have run out or the evader may have been separated from his kit.

Magnifying glass. This is another good method of lighting a fire and it will not wear out. Angle the glass appropriately to catch the sun's rays and focus it on some dry tinder, paper or grass. It should first smoke, then glow red, after which, with a little gentle blowing, it may burst into flame.

Flint. A typical survival kit may include a small saw and a small metal bar. Draw the saw across the bar to produce a spark over some dry grass or similar. Alternatively, strike a piece of flint stone with metal.

Bow and drill. Make a bow with some willow and stretch a string across it, end to end. Make a drill by sharpening one end of a stick and leaving the other end rounded. Take a fist-sized piece of wood and hollow a rounded area into the centre so it can hold the rounded end of the stick. Place the pointed end of the drill on a wood block near some dry tinder and pull the bow to and fro so that it turns the stick.

Hand drill. Take a stick and rub it between your hands so that it turns very swiftly on a block of wood near some tinder. Eventually, the wood and tinder should start to smoke and catch fire.

Fire Plough. Cut a groove in some soft wood and then use a hard wood stick to plough up and down it until the friction produces enough heat to ignite the small slithers of wood that have been produced by the ploughing action. Have some dry grass on hand or something similar to encourage the flame.

Fire Plough

This is one of a variety of friction methods designed to produce heat and a flame. The stick pushed rapidly up and down the groove produces heat.

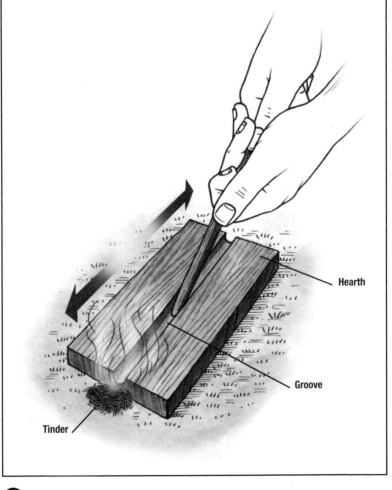

Hearth

Groove

Tinder

Hand Drill

By spinning a stick rapidly in a groove, you may be able to produce enough heat through friction to light some dry tinder.

Making your own Compass

Although small compasses can be hidden in buttons and elsewhere, and should be part of an escape kit, the evader may have been stripped of everything.

If the evader can find a metallic object, such as a sewing needle, he can break it in half, and use one half to form the direction pointer and the other half the pivot. The pivot point should be pushed through the bottom of a container. To counterbalance the needle pointer, attach something like the nib of a pen, with either glue or gum, or sap from a tree.

Another method is to suspend a razor blade from a hair or piece of string. To magnetize the metal, stroke it one way on a piece of silk.

Metal can also be polarized by the use of a magnet, stroking it in one direction only.

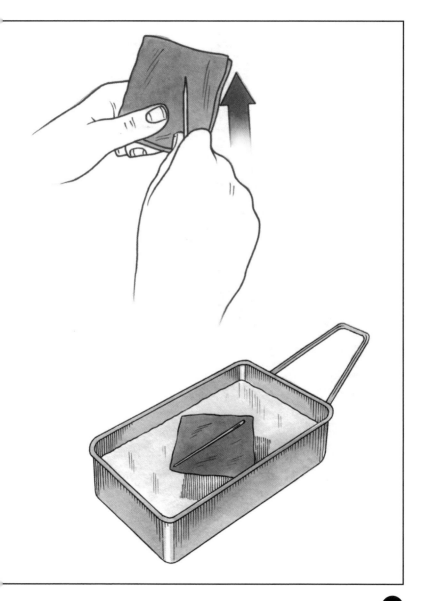

CASE STUDY 2:

Classic Manhunts

Daniel Boone Rescues his Daughter

Daniel Boone (c. 1734–1820) is one of the iconic figures of the early American frontier. Born of an English Quaker family from Devon, Boone would help to open up the route through the Cumberland Gap into Kentucky, which proved to be a favourite hunting ground for Boone, although the Shawnee Indians regarded it as exclusively theirs. Once they captured Boone, they stripped him of all his skins and told him never to return.

The continual disputes with the Indians sometimes resulted in shocking atrocities, as the Indians tried to terrorize the settlers and force them to leave. In this they had some success. As part of this programme of terror, in 1776, a Shawnee raiding party captured Boone's own teenage daughter Jemma and two other girls. There was no doubt in Boone's mind as to what might happen to his daughter, for his son, James, had previously been captured by the Shawnee, tortured and murdered.

Although the Shawnee had a lead on him of at least two days, Boone summoned all of the tracking skills that he had learned over the years as a hunter and frontiersman to make sure he found his daughter. Eventually, he caught up with her captors and turned the tables on them. The hunters had become the hunted and this time the Indians were ambushed and Boone rescued the three girls.

It is said that the girls attempted to leave evidence on the trail to make it easier for the rescuers to find them, and it is not unlikely that Boone and his companions might have been able to pick up a bit of torn dress or some other evidence to add to their other tracking clues.

Geronimo

Geronimo (1829–1909) was a chief of the Chiricahua Apache. After his mother, wife and children were killed by Mexicans, Geronimo embarked on a series of revenge raids, aimed primarily at Mexicans. After the United States forcibly moved 4,000 Apaches to a reservation, Geronimo led the fightback, which resulted in a series of intense and vicious battles and raids.

Eventually Geronimo was defeated by forces led by Lt.-Col. George F. Crook and surrendered in January 1884. However, Geronimo was not the type to sit quietly in a reservation for the rest of his days, and in May 1885 he escaped, along with a band of followers.

Geronimo was on the loose again and a massive manhunt was organized to find him. Captain Henry Lawton, commanding B Troop, 4th Cavalry at Fort Huachuca, and Lt. Charles B. Gatewood, commander of Indian scouts, were to lead the manhunt. They were both experienced Indian fighters, and Gatewood in particular, as a commander of Indian scouts, was familiar with Indian ways and was in return respected by the Indians.

Nevertheless, the hunt for Geronimo would take about a year and would pit the Apaches – people with an innate sense of the land and a genius for being able to appear or disappear at will – against the dogged determination of American soldiers who had learned many of their skills from the very people they were now pursuing. Gatewood himself had taken care both to learn the Apache language and to gain their acceptance. He had had the humility, rare among American officers of his day, to learn from the native people he was commanding. He knew that, although he was a graduate of West Point and knew many of the arts of war, he was inferior to the Apaches in many areas, including their superior tracking and scouting skills. So great was the respect that the Apaches had for Gatewood that their Chief Geronimo himself told him: 'You can come to our camp anywhere … Never fear harm.'

So the manhunt that eventually tracked down Geronimo was conducted by an experienced scout who had largely learned his trade from Indians and by Indian scouts themselves.

Reinhard Heydrich and Special Operations Executive (SOE)

Reinhard Heydrich (1904–42) almost makes Osama bin Laden seem like an amateur. He had the suave appearance of a civilized member of the German middle class, being the son of a cultured

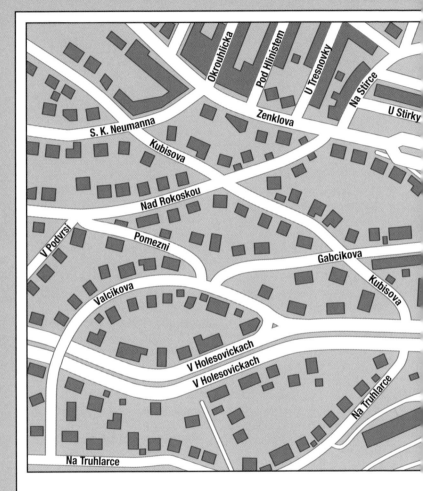

Wagnerian musician, and yet he was considered the most dangerous man in Germany after Hitler. Even members of the Nazi Party feared him.

When he was appointed Reich Protector of Bohemia and Moravia in 1941, Heydrich's 'charm offensive' included both mass executions and economic

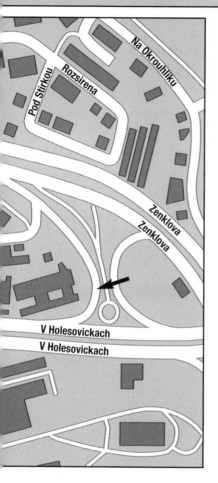

The Holesovice intersection in Prague where Richard Heydrich was intercepted by SOE agents.

the Czechs that no one would dare attack him, so he drove in an open Mercedes with only a chauffeur as an escort, and took the same route to and from his office every day.

The operation to hunt down Heydrich and kill him was organized in England by the Czech military intelligence and by the British Special Operations Executive (SOE). On 29 December 1941, two Czech SOE agents, Jan Kubiš and Jozef Gabčík, were dropped into Czechoslovakia by an RAF Halifax bomber of 138 Squadron.

On 27 May, the agents moved to a road intersection at Holesovice where there was a hairpin bend that would force Heydrich's car to slow down. There was a tram stop nearby where Kubiš stood with a Sten Gun hidden under a raincoat. When Gabčík signalled that Heydrich's car was on the way, Kubiš assessed the street and waited by the corner with his Sten. As the car slowed, he dropped his raincoat, pointed the Sten Gun and pulled the trigger, but the gun jammed. Heydrich saw what had happened, told the driver to stop

initiatives to pacify the Czechs. His apparent success led to a false sense of security that was to prove his fatal mistake. He imagined that he had so terrorized

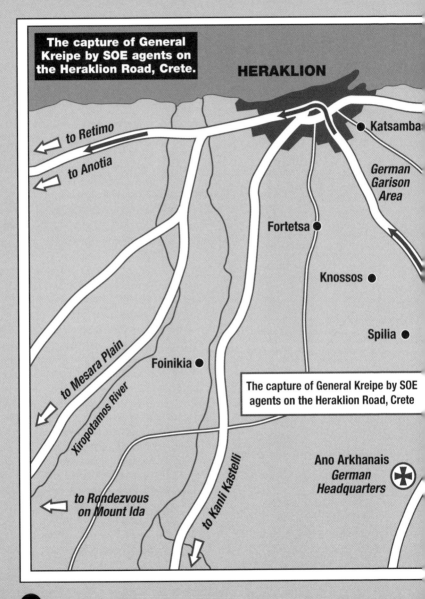

The capture of General Kreipe by SOE agents on the Heraklion Road, Crete.

HERAKLION

to Retimo

to Anotia

Katsamba

German Garison Area

Fortetsa

Knossos

Spilia

to Mesara Plain

Xiropotamos River

Foinikia

The capture of General Kreipe by SOE agents on the Heraklion Road, Crete

to Rondezvous on Mount Ida

to Kanli Kastelli

Ano Arkhanais German Headquarters

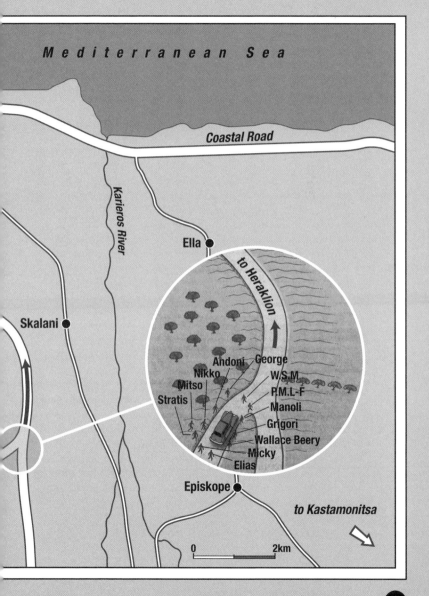

Mediterranean Sea

Coastal Road

Karieros River

Ella

to Heraklion

Skalani

Andoni   George
Nikko   W.S.M
Mitso   P.M.L-F
Stratis   Manoli
                  Grigori
                  Wallace Beery
                  Micky
Elias

Episkope

to Kastamonitsa

0   2km

and stood up with his pistol. This gave Kubiš the chance he needed. He threw a bomb at the car but it hit the rear wheel, where it exploded, mortally wounding Heydrich.

Although the evidence left on the street, including a British Sten Gun and British-made plastic explosives, pointed directly to a British operation, Hitler ordered reprisals, including the destruction of the village of Lidice, where all the men were shot, the women sent to concentration camps and the children taken away to be 'Germanized'. The village itself was burnt to the ground.

The manhunt had now turned round. The SOE agents were hunted unsuccessfully until a Czech SOE agent betrayed them and they were traced to the catacombs of an Orthodox Church and, after an intensive battle, they committed suicide.

Capture of General Kreipe on the Island of Crete

After the British had lost the island of Crete to the Germans in 1941, a ruthless regime was put in place under General Friedrich-Wilhelm Müller. In view of his brutality, SOE planned to abduct him and take him to Egypt. To avoid reprisals

against the Cretans, they planned to ensure that the operation was obviously carried out by British commandos. By the time the operation was mounted, Müller had been replaced by General Heinrich Kreipe, but it was decided to go ahead anyway. The two primary SOE agents were Major Patrick Leigh-Fermor and Captain William Stanley Moss. They were backed by a team that included other SOE agents as well as Cretan resistance fighters.

General Kreipe travelled alone in his car with his chauffeur. Leigh-Fermor and Moss disguised themselves as German military police and flagged down the car before ripping open the doors and knocking out the driver with a cosh. The ambushers then had to drive the car through 22 German checkpoints.

Soon the hunters became the hunted as the Germans started to comb the island on foot and by air, also dropping pamphlets threatening reprisals against the local population if General Kreipe was not returned. The British officers, Cretan fighters and their hostage had to find their way over the mountains of Crete with the aid of scouts to rendezvous with a Royal Navy ship that would take them to Egypt. They hid in old shepherds' huts or in caves.

After some searching, they found a secluded beach, which was not watched by a German sentry post, and sent a Morse code signal to be picked up. Eventually, a boat arrived filled with British Commandos looking for a fight and very disappointed to discover that there were no Germans in the area.

British SAS in Borneo

When the Federation of Malaya was created by the amalgamation of Sabah and Sarawak in British Borneo in 1963, there were regular border clashes involving Indonesian forces who opposed the new arrangement.

A Squadron 22 SAS under Major John Edwardes was sent to Borneo to help seal the border. Since the border was 1500km (930 miles) long, this was a challenging assignment. However, the SAS knew that their best allies in this particular mission were the local tribespeople, who knew the country like the back of their hand.

The SAS spread 21 patrols along the length of the border, and each patrol worked on building positive relations with local villages. The SAS men would visit the villages to help with medical problems and building projects. Gradually, a mutual trust was built up. The villagers provided trackers and other essential knowledge of the area. By this method, the relatively small number of SAS four-man patrols had in effect an army of expert trackers at their disposal, while the local natives provided key intelligence on enemy movements.

The SAS themselves were to act as guides and trackers for larger units of regular forces when the occasion required. The British began to send missions across the border to put the Indonesians on the back foot under Operation 'Claret'. The Special Boat Service also performed raids up the various rivers.

The main tactic was to set up ambushes for Indonesian forces. This required extremely high levels of jungle skills by the SAS and their trackers, as they had to move into position unseen and have an accurate knowledge of likely enemy movements.

The SAS in Borneo ran a successful counter-insurgency operation against Indonesian forces.

Timeline

14 July 1776: Jemima Boone and two other teenage girls captured by Shawnee war party. Daniel Boone sets out on their trail, eventually tracking them down and rescuing the girls.

May 1885: Apache Chief Geronimo escapes from imprisonment with a band of followers.

4 September 1886: Geronimo and his band surrender to US forces after a lengthy manhunt.

29 December 1941: Two Czech SOE agents fly from England and parachute into Czechoslovakia to track down and assassinate Nazi leader Reinhard Heydrich.

27 May 1942: The SOE agents throw a bomb at Heydrich's car, mortally wounding him.

26 April 1944: SOE agents Major Patrick Leigh-Fermor and Captain William Stanley Moss abduct General Kreipe, commander of German forces on the island of Crete.

14 May 1944: The SOE team and the General are picked up by a British motor launch and taken to Egypt.

Early 1963: British SAS squadron arrives on island of Borneo to patrol border of Sarawak against Indonesian insurgency.

July 1964–July 1966: Operation 'Claret' involves the SAS and other units from the UK and allies, including Australia and New Zealand, in cross-border patrols to deter Indonesian insurgency.

One of the first things that may be noticed about an experienced tracker is their obvious familiarity with their surroundings. A tracker may be someone who either tracks for a living, such as a Scottish ghillie or another type of gamekeeper, or is involved with a professional organization such as the Scouts, or is perhaps a member of the armed forces. The underlying principle of familiarity with your surroundings is that you are attuned to the ways of nature and are sensitive to unexpected changes.

Mindset of a Tracker

Somebody who spends a lot of time outdoors tends to have more highly attuned senses and a sharper awareness of movement, sounds and smells. Those who met individuals such as Frederick Russell Burnham (see p66) or Frederick Courteney Selous (see p25) commented on the clarity of their eyes, accustomed to gazing over wide open spaces.

When outdoors, natural instincts are being developed that are not required or used when living in an urban environment. Apart from

. . . .

Tracking and field craft involve a wide range of skills, including observational skills and patience as well as a good knowledge of camouflage and concealment.

Tracking in the field involves many of the skills that hunters have practised for thousands of years.

Principles of Tracking in the Field

ally
no signs
in the
d the lie
to living
e of
seeking
o the
subtle sounds of nature and noticing its movements, the person used to living outdoors develops an instinctive understanding of nature.

A typical urban person is to some degree overwhelmed with stimuli, including advertising, whether on the TV, the computer or on the street, the noise of cars or other machines and maybe rather uninteresting urban odours. As a result, the tendency may be for the senses to try to blank out some of these stimuli to avoid sensory overload. The tendency to blank out unpleasant urban sounds and replace them with selected good ones can sometimes be seen when people carry personal music systems and earphones. This is understandable in the city but it is strange to see walkers or runners with earphones in the countryside. They do not seem to realize that the occasional sounds of birds, of the wind in the trees or of water in a stream are pleasant to the ear and part of the overall sensation of nature. Apart from anything else, listening to these sounds and gazing at beautiful natural landscapes can have a very calming effect.

Natural Senses

Simple activities such as countryside walking can help to re-tune the natural senses, making them sharper, and you more aware of the natural clues used by trackers.

An urbanized person is used to bright colours grabbing his attention in advertising and other media. A country person is used to more muted and subtle colourations and is able to gaze so that he can detect objects and movements beyond what is immediately visible. The average city-dweller will also not take much

notice of the movement of wildlife, least of all birds, partly because their occasional appearance during the day or night is largely meaningless. The only way to understand their pattern of behaviour is to observe them carefully and quietly over a period of time. So if you are used to an urban environment, it may be a good idea to get out into the countryside and watch and listen in order to develop and tune your senses. This will help you to be a better tracker.

Birdwatchers sometimes choose a patch of ground that they regularly return to in order to record what is going on among the bird and other

City Walking

Walking around a big city means being surrounded by noise and bustle that tend to overwhelm and dull the senses. However, a modern manhunt will often require the ability to track an evader in urban environments.

animal populations. Although to some extent this may seem as odd as trainspotting, regular, patient observation brings the reward of understanding patterns of behaviour and providing deeper insights into the natural world. As with most things, once you begin to scratch the surface, you want to know more. So an experienced naturalist or country person will have an understanding of what a particular bird is doing in a hedgerow at a particular time of year, whereas to the casual passer-by it is just a bird.

Good trackers will probably be both mentally and physically fit. Apart from having highly attuned senses, they will also be making intelligent deductions. Trackers need to be intuitive and to understand what an animal or human is likely to have done in the circumstances. They will often be bending down, stopping and starting, in order to examine tracks and other evidence, and they will also need to be agile. They will need to have a high level of attention to detail in order to be able to discern small clues and not just rush past them, impatient to get ahead. They will need constantly to be asking themselves what something means when a casual passer-by might dismiss it as irrelevant. They also need to have endurance and the ability to recognize when they are tired and no longer able to discern or interpret clues.

Physically Demanding

A tracker needs to be both patient and physically fit, as the work involves a lot of painstaking checking for small clues on the ground and in the surrounding environment.

Examining Clues

A tracker will examine plants in the area of the hunt for clues such as broken twigs or bits of material that may have been caught in foliage and so on.

A good tracker may to some extent adopt the qualities of an artist. To a casual passer-by, a tree is just a tree, though they may make some judgment as to whether it is beautiful or not. To an artist, a tree is a collection of shapes, the main focus of which may be the pattern of the bark, the outline of branches and twigs or the arrangement of leaves. The main point is that by steady observation the artist notices things about an object that simply would not be seen by someone glancing at it.

For hunters from early times to the present, where they still exist in some parts of Africa, Borneo, Indonesia and South America, there is one overriding instinct that concentrates the mind and all the senses – hunger. It may sufficiently concentrate the mind of modern man to get down to the local supermarket if there is nothing in the freezer but there are not many skills involved in that. For the hunter who relies on meat to survive, every sense is tuned to its maximum to ensure the success of the chase. Modern trackers have in some way to simulate that fine-tuning and urgency rather than casually passing over essential detailed clues while dreaming of the hamburger and chips they will be having for lunch.

Stalking and Stealth

Animals have highly tuned senses to help them survive. Even in countries where animals such as deer no

Scottish Ghillies and the Lovat Scouts

Scottish ghillies are famed throughout the world for their skills and knowledge with regard to approaching animals, mainly red deer in the Scottish highlands. One famous ghillie was John Brown, who was a close personal attendant of Queen Victoria.

In 1900, during the Second Boer War, a new unit of scouts was formed by Simon Fraser, 14th Lord Lovat. The unit was commanded by an American, Major Frederick Russell Burnham, who, as mentioned previously in this book, was a highly experienced scout who learned his skills on the American frontier. The Lovat Scouts used many of the skills that are now regularly taught to Boy Scouts, including tracking. For scouts, as with Special Forces, the skill was to stay alive.

Later, in World War I, a unit of sharpshooters or snipers was formed, consisting largely of ghillies from Highland estates. These men had a natural aptitude for sniping, which requires covert movement and extreme patience; and they were also masters of camouflage. The Lovat Scouts' sharpshooters used the ghillie suit, variations of which are still used by snipers today.

A nephew of Simon Fraser was David Stirling, who founded the Special Air Service (SAS).

Deer Alert

Animals such as deer have highly tuned hearing as well as sense of smell. The principles of tracking animals can also be used when tracking humans.

longer have natural predators, they remain as wary and as alert as ever to the slightest movement, sound or scent. Herbivores such as deer have eyes on the side of their heads, which give them good side and rear vision, and also large upright ears that pick up sounds very quickly. They are often long-legged and can run at great speed.

The alertness of animals such as deer provides a challenge for deer stalkers. Sportsmen who wish to shoot deer are often accompanied by an experienced ghillie who guides them in the subtle arts of approaching an animal without being seen, heard or smelled.

Camouflage and Concealment

Animals are masters of camouflage and over time many species have adapted to their surroundings, such as a deer blending in with brown bracken. An arctic hare is barely discernible in the snow, and the spots of a leopard make it very difficult to make out its shape from a distance. Although the stripes on a zebra may seem to make it stand out from the brown African savannah, rather than blending in, when the zebras are galloping in a stampede, the stripes have a mesmerizing and confusing effect on predators such as lions.

Likewise, to approach animals successfully or to remain hidden from human targets, camouflage is

MARPAT

Military forces such as the US Marines have adopted sophisticated disruptive camouflage patterns that result from the application of high technology.

Altering Shadows

Becoming aware of shadows is a key component of concealment, as the human shadow is very distinct. The effect can be reduced by camouflage that disrupts shape.

required, always bearing in mind the particular nature of the surroundings. Military forces often issue different styles of camouflage uniforms for different climate regions, including temperate, desert, jungle and arctic. Trackers should likewise wear either disruptive-pattern clothing or some shade of green or brown to provide some measure of concealment in the relevant environment.

Some military forces are also issued urban camouflage uniforms. Scientific approaches to camouflage have resulted, for example, in the US Marines Corps MARine PATern (MARPAT) uniform, which is created by a large number of rectangular pixels of colour. This camouflage pattern is also known as a digital pattern and was created in association with the US Marines Scout Sniper School.

One of the considerations that had to be taken into account when designing MARPAT was the distinction between primary and secondary vision. When using secondary vision, people make an association between what they see and a preconceived mental image of what they should be seeing. Using secondary vision, someone may be staring straight at an object but fail to notice it because it does not correspond to what it should look like. When using primary vision, people analyze their environment with a clean sheet and try to work out what they are actually

seeing as opposed to what they should be seeing. As mentioned before, this is what artists are often taught to do – to draw or paint what they see rather than draw, say, a chair or a vase. They forget what the object intrinsically is and what it should look like in order to focus on the shape in the particular conditions presented to them. For example, people using secondary vision looking into a forest or field of bracken may be thinking 'deer' and try to find a shape that corresponds. They will probably fail because the deer's camouflage is designed to conceal their shape by blending with their surroundings. Someone using primary vision, however, will be looking for visual clues that help them discern something present that is not part of the background. Like someone finding pieces in a jigsaw puzzle, they may see something that indicates an ear or a tail, for example, and work from there.

The other consideration when it comes to producing effective camouflage is how nature works versus how humans work. Nature often produces random patterns, especially in mixed foliage, for example, whereas humans tend to produce patterns in regular repeated forms. The ghillie suit is more advanced in this respect, as the pattern tends to be random. Careful analysis, however, may pick out a regular uniform pattern against

Camouflage Helmet

Camouflage on a helmet can help disrupt the shape of the helmet and head. Care must be taken to ensure that the camouflage matches the environment.

Multi-Terrain Pattern

The British Army developed a new camouflage that would provide optimum balance for military personnel operating in both wooded and arid environments.

random background foliage. Another danger is that the camouflage pattern may seem to coalesce when seen from a distance, thereby failing in its disruptive effect.

The ideal camouflage is one that makes the wearer as closely identified with the background as possible; and to achieve this the positive form of the person needs to be reduced as much as possible. Apart from regular patterns, humans tend to produce primary colours, as opposed to the muted colours of nature. When assigned to produce a uniform mixing green and brown, for example, the colours often tend to be true green and true brown. These will stand out from the authentic natural environment, which has more muted colours that reflect light off each other in very subtle ways. Standard camouflage patterns tend to be in blocks of colour that look good when on the hanger in a shop but stick out a mile in a natural environment.

The thinking behind this (big blocks of colour do not really work) is also verified by the British Army, which replaced its 40-year-old Disruptive Pattern Material (DPM) with a new Multi-Terrain Pattern (MTP). Not only are the colours more subtle and less solid in the MTP uniform, they are also more adaptable. For example, British forces fighting in Afghanistan found themselves shifting between desert-like conditions and a green zone.

Bin Laden latest:

Why is the rubbish burned outside the house rather than being put out for collection?

The MTP Pattern was based on a scientifically created pattern developed initially for Special Forces. The British Army retained the purely desert combat uniform for relevant assignments. The MTP pattern was part of a wider programme for UK armed forces known as the Personal Clothing System.

Movement

As animals and snipers know: however well camouflaged you are, you can easily give away your position by moving. Animals often freeze when in danger so as to minimize this possibility. Snipers know that they have to allow a great deal of time to get into position and that their movements have to be sloth like. They will often also move only under cover of darkness.

Although the human eye is good at spotting movement, depending on the conditions, subtle movements

Attracting Attention

When practising evasion or pursuing a target in a covert way, it is especially important to be aware of how not to attract attention by, for example, the bright face of a watch or a pale human face, by standing out in the open and creating a silhouette, or even by rapid movement.

A flash of reflected sunlight

The human outline

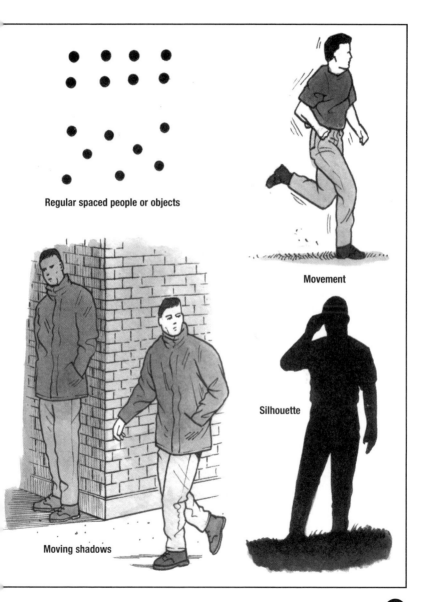

Regular spaced people or objects

Movement

Silhouette

Moving shadows

Camouflaging Skin

The principle of camouflage is to disrupt shapes that the human eye will instinctively recognize. The 'blotch' pattern here is ideally suited to temperate deciduous (leaf-shedding) areas, deserts and barren, snowy landscapes.

The 'slash' pattern of camouflage is specifically designed for coniferous, jungle and grassy areas, the long, contrasting stripes down the face blending in with the vertical lines of the surrounding vegetation.

Blending In

Blending in to the environment can involve an instinctive use of natural features to minimize the exposure of the human body. Adopt a pose that mimics the shape of the features around you: stand upright against a tree, lay flat along a horizontal branch or sit down among boulders on a hillside.

Sniper in a Ghillie Suit

The ghillie suit was created by Scottish ghillies or gamekeepers for deer stalking. It has been developed by military forces to provide camouflage for snipers and other personnel operating in a covert way. Here, a sniper is barely visible amongst the vegetation.

may be difficult to detect or may be interpreted wrongly. When looking at something directly, the brain tends to interpret the movement. Sometimes this interpretation may be faulty and there may then be a failure to react. When movement is picked up by the peripheral vision, however, there is less interpretation and more of a reflex response to the movement.

The Ghillie Suit

The ghillie suit was originally devised by Scottish ghillies, or hunting attendants, in the Scottish highlands, to break up the human form when approaching wildlife. It is often constructed around netting and is covered in loose, leaf-like material. The user may add bits of real local foliage to the ghillie suit in order to blend in optimally with the surroundings, though care has to be taken to ensure vegetation remains fresh and does not look out of place. The ragged outlines of the ghillie suit make it very difficult for either the human or animal eye to make out the human form and the eye soon tires of the effort.

Tracking Stick

A tracking stick is used by trackers to provide easy measurement of tracks across a number of planes. It can be up to 1.23m (4ft) long and can either be marked with notches to show measurements or have rubber rings or elastic bands to put round it.

The tracker will measure the length of stride of a person or animal from heel to heel or, alternatively, whichever part of the print is most visible. For animals, this may in fact be the claw marks at the front of the footprint.

Once the tracker has measured a typical stride, he can use this to help him deduce where the next track should be in places where the track is no longer obvious. There may be an area of hard ground, for example, where the track suddenly disappears. By knowing where it should be, however, the tracker can search for other clues, for example a disturbed pebble or vegetation of some kind. Once the clue is found, the tracker can carry on with the stick or make suitable deductions about the direction of the animal's or person's route so as to be able to continue tracking.

A sophisticated tracking stick will not only be used to measure the length of stride but also other aspects of the pattern of a track.

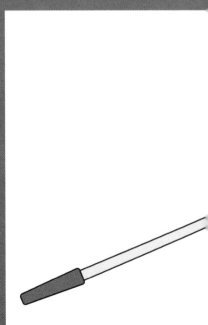

For example, these can include:
- Tip of stick to first mark – to measure length.
- First mark to second mark – to measure width of stride.
- Tip of stick to third mark – to measure the stride.
- Third mark to fourth mark – to measure the straddle (or distance between the feet on the ground).
- Fourth mark to fifth mark – to measure the pitch or angle of the footprint away from the direction of travel.

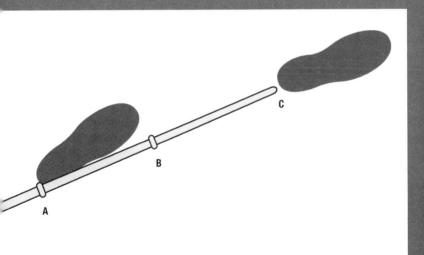

If you wag your finger in front of your face, you can almost hear yourself thinking 'that's a finger wagging'. If you wag your finger on the edge of your peripheral vision, to the left or right of your head, there is a greater tendency to react to the movement rather than interpret it.

A reactive, non-interpretative way of seeing movement can be useful in situations where a tired mind may not be drawing the right conclusions. However, sometimes movement may need to be interpreted. For example, if grass or leaves are swaying and there is no wind, it may be because an animal or a human is moving them. Other intuitive ways of detecting movement are to look out for shadows or to detect the movement of other wildlife that may have been frightened by the movement of something or someone near them.

A very easy way of both detecting movement and of giving away your own position is reflection. You may be well camouflaged but the sun may glint off your watch face. Military-style watches often have darkened faces and bodies for this reason. If you have binoculars, these can easily reflect light, and the same can be said for a telescopic sight on a rifle. Not only the sun but strong moonlight can also be reflected.

Again, you may be wearing excellent camouflage clothing but making yourself obvious by visible pale skin on your face, hands or arms. Military forces are experts in camouflaging skin with 'camo cream'. The ideal is to have a base layer to take away the shine, followed by blotches of darker colour (brown, green and black) to break up the lines of the face.

Scent

Because the human sense of smell is comparatively limited, it is easy to forget that animals often have a highly acute sense of smell and are regularly sifting through a whole library of smells and distinguishing between them.

You can invest in the best camouflage equipment and your silent movement may be faultless, but if you are upwind of an animal, you might as well strut about in a loud Hawaiian shirt. A tracker dog can detect a man at a considerable distance. The ability to use the sense of smell is not limited to dogs, however. In the Malaysian jungle and in Vietnam, British and American soldiers were sometimes detected by native villagers or insurgents because of their use of scented soaps and aftershave.

Habits

An experienced ghillie or tracker will not only know about approach methods and signs of the presence of a person, he will also have an intuitive understanding of likely reactions. This is a very powerful tool when tracking.

Displacement

Apart from following tracks, the tracker will also be on the lookout for signs of displacement, such as water on rocks, mud on vegetation and sand on grass.

Mud on vegetation

Water on rocks

Sand on grass

Likewise, when tracking a human, you can make deductions about what they are likely to have done in particular circumstances. As you are a human yourself, ask yourself which way you would have gone when, say, confronted by a particular obstacle and what you would have done if you wanted to evade a tracker.

Shape

While writing this chapter, I went out for an evening walk in the rain down to our local river. As I walked along the towpath, I heard a snort and looked across the river in the gloom to see a large, looming black shape in the gloom. The size of the shape, the fact that it made an animal-like snort and the fact that I knew cattle often grazed in the fields on the other side of the river made me think initially that I was looking at either a cow or a bull. As I tried to discern the shape, I noticed it did not move and that it was somewhat shapeless for a cow. Then I realized that, in fact, I was looking at a large fisherman's umbrella and that the snort came from the fisherman, who was sitting underneath it.

I was, of course, all the time trying to make logical connections between the shape and the surroundings, and what might or should have been there. As I walked further along the towpath, more shapes loomed out of the darkness, still somewhat formless but upright. I worked out that these

Types of Footprint

The spacing of footprints can reveal much about the person being pursued and whether they were walking, running, tired, carrying a heavy object and so on.

1. **Someone running (long strides).**

2. **Someone carrying a heavy load (feet drag between steps).**

3. **A person wearing military-style boots.**

4. **A woman in stilettoes.**

5. **Someone walking backwards.**

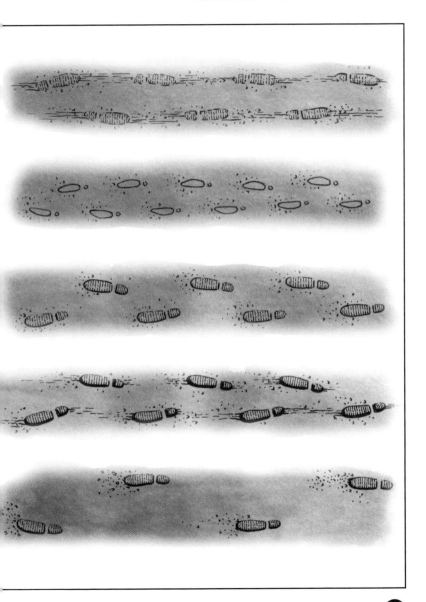

were fishermen standing in heavy waterproofs that concealed most of the shape of their bodies.

In each case my interpretative skills were challenged by what my eyes were picking up because, of course, you need to come to some sort of conclusion about what you are seeing, especially in a situation where what you are seeing may pose some kind of threat to you. If you do not see what you expect to see, where you expect to see it, you will be surprised by how hard you have to work to make out what the shape actually is. If you are tired, the mind can almost give up completely and tell you that you are 'seeing things'.

Take the example of a Special Forces soldier who has been out all night on an army exercise, perhaps carrying a heavy bergen and a weapon. The next morning he has to stay awake to provide a sentry watch for his four-man squad. He sees, or thinks he does, someone in a gas mask and the barrel of a rifle very close to him. He does not know whether to call out or fire his weapon, because he is not entirely sure what he is seeing is real. These kinds of challenges can be presented as tired minds try to interpret messages the eyes may or may not be sending them. The slow approach of a sniper in a ghillie suit, therefore, can fool even the most watchful sentry, because the mind has no information to interpret anything out of the ordinary.

Sign

The evidence left by an animal or human as it passes through an area is known as a 'sign'. This includes the track or footprints as well as other evidence, such as small hairs or threads from clothing, disturbed foliage, broken twigs and so on. The term 'spoor' includes both visual signs, such as tracks, as well as the scent of an animal or human or of anything they have left behind, such as dung or a campfire. Visual sign can be divided into ground sign and top sign.

Ground sign

Ground sign, as the term obviously suggests, is usually found on the ground or near it. It includes every clue left behind by an animal or human, and there is almost no limit to what ground sign can be. Obvious examples are tracks themselves, flattened or broken vegetation, disturbed stones, animal deposits, remnants of hair or clothing fibres, and any form of litter, such as a sweet wrapper or a matchstick.

Expert trackers can go beyond these obvious signs and make deductions that are often extremely subtle. For example, a stone or pebble that has been knocked out of the way by an animal is no longer present, but it may have left its evidence in the form of a small deposit of earth that has collected around it and which remains as evidence.

Trackers can also deduce how long ago something or someone has passed through an area by examining, for example, how green a broken twig or branch is, or how warm are the embers of a fire.

Top sign

Top sign is similar to ground sign but is generally seen above knee level and includes marks on the sides of trees, broken spider webs, grass that is leaning forward because something has brushed through it, and balls of hair caught on wire. Animals sometimes claw at trees or gnaw on branches. When an animal disturbs something at a certain height, it can indicate the animal's height and size.

Tracks

Tracks are the signatures by which a variety of animals can easily be recognized and they can also provide easy recognition for humans who may be wearing shoes with a distinctive tread. Expert trackers go well beyond the recognition of tracks left by different kinds of animal. They can also make a whole range of other deductions, which can include the size and weight of an animal, whether or not it is injured, the speed at which it was travelling and the sort of mood it was in (i.e. whether relaxed or agitated).

Expert trackers will often carry with them a tracking stick, which allows them to measure such features as the stride length, the straddle and so on.

Measuring Tracks

Measurable track characteristics include:

A – Length
B – Width
C – Stride Length
D – Straddle
E – Pitch

Human Footprints

A human footprint made by someone walking at a normal pace is characterized by an initial heel strike, full pressure of the foot on the ground, a roll-through to the ball of the foot and then a final toe-off.

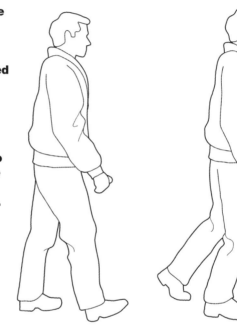

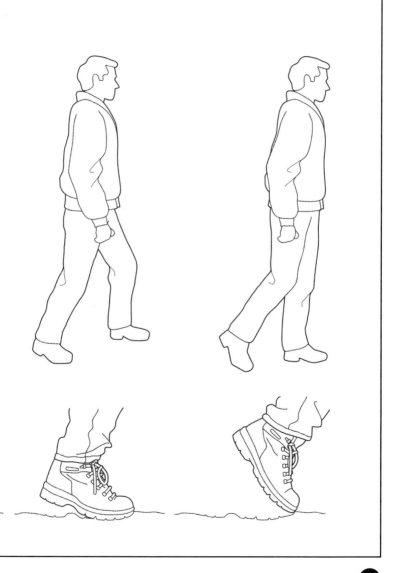

Backtracking

Backtracking is a method of fooling a tracker by moving back on the footprints you have made before heading off in another direction. An expert tracker may spot this evasion technique.

Identifying footprints and what they mean

There is more than meets the eye in a human footprint. The obvious thing to notice is the type of tread and whether it is consistent and fits the type used by the quarry. However, there are other clues that can be deduced by studying the print.

If the quarry is barefoot, there are various ways of identifying the foot, such as the space between the toes and also the amount of pressure formed by the instep, which is known as 'pronation'.

If the quarry is wearing footwear, there are a whole range of clues that will identify the print, such as any peculiarities in the tread (i.e. where a piece of tread is worn or missing), the length and breadth of the footwear, name or numbers on the side of the shoe and so on.

The length of stride can also be measured (and from this the height of the person deduced), though this will vary according to the speed with which the quarry is moving.

It may be apparent whether the quarry is male or female, according to the size of the footwear.

Walking and running action

When walking, the foot naturally rolls through a step, and the most obviously marked areas in the foot cycle are the outer side of the back of the heel as well as the inner side of the toe. Also, the ball of the foot behind the big toe tends to make a marked impression.

The type of impression varies according to the speed at which the person is walking. When walking slowly, the feet tend to be splayed outwards to maintain balance. If the person starts to trot or run, the pace should lengthen and the footmarks will appear to be straight. This is because there is more balance in the forward movement and momentum. In a full run, there may only be signs of the forward part of the foot showing on the ground.

Experienced trackers will be able to recognize when the quarry is trying to fool them by walking backwards. One of the signs is that in order to propel backwards, the person will push off with the heel. This should be obvious from the marked heel impression on the ground.

A person carrying a load may be identified by relatively short steps with deep indentations and a slightly erratic path. An erratic path may also be an indication of tiredness or even exhaustion, which is a very useful clue for the tracker. Depending on the level of exhaustion, the tracks may even cross over each other, showing a stumbling, shambling gait.

Tracks will also indicate such things as whether the person has an injury, where there will be a disproportionate indentation made

Assessing Foot Traffic

By marking out a particular area, it is possible to make an assessment of the number of people who have passed through an area, and also gauge their size.

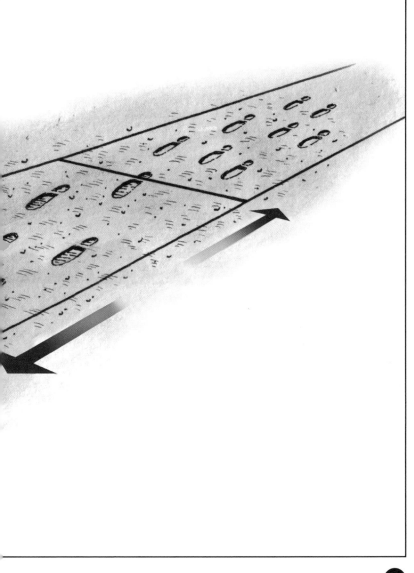

by a healthy leg as opposed to a light mark made by an injured one.

You may come to an area of hard ground or rock where a human would expect to lose a tracker. In such areas, you can use your tracking skills to work out the likely position of tracks and you may also need to examine the ground with particular care from close range. Sometimes, it can help to actually place your head horizontally on the ground or rock and look across the surface. You may then be able to notice small undulations indicating the presence of a track that cannot be seen from above.

As you move on, make sure you scan the area around the last sign systematically, ready to notice any small disturbances on the ground and allowing your eyes time to really see what is there.

Tracking clues

It is one thing identifying a track, but it is quite another to make the right deductions about what it means, as

Getting into Position

Sometimes, on hard ground for instance, a track can only be spotted from the side, as opposed to from the top, as small amounts of piled-up debris can then be seen.

each and every track has a range of clues hidden within it.

One way of judging the age of a track is whether it has been affected by rain. You can normally tell this if the track has evidence of raindrops or has been partially washed away. By working out when it last rained, you can judge the age of the track. An experienced tracker will make deductions about the state and colour of bent grass. After a certain amount of time, grass that has been bent will change colour. The age of tracks in mud or damp ground can be calculated by the extent to which water has seeped into the track, and the condition of the mud that has been forced upwards by the impression of the foot or knocked away from the damp area and left to dry.

Another way of calculating the age of a track is the amount of debris that has collected on it and also whether any animal tracks have passed over it. As animals tend to move at night, this provides a clue as to how old the track is.

Lost Track Drill

Military units such as the Selous Scouts, as well as civilian trackers, sometimes use rehearsed methods for occasions where the track or spoor is lost and it is unclear which direction to continue in.

360-Degree Search Method

With this method, the tracker will continue forward for a few paces to check whether he can pick up the trail in the original direction of march. If the spoor is still not found, the tracker returns to the point where the last spoor was seen and begins a series of 360-degree searches around the last spoor, in ever-widening circles. This continues until another spoor is found.

Box Method

Another method of searching for lost spoor from the point of the last spoor is the box method. Here, the tracker continues forward for about 200m (656ft), turns right for about 100m (328ft) and then returns back to the baseline of the last spoor. Once he reaches the point of the last spoor, he repeats the exercise, this time turning left before returning.

Cross-Grain Search Pattern

The cross-grain search method is another variant on searching for a lost spoor. Here, the tracker carries on for about 150m (492ft) to check whether he can pick up the spoor again on the same line of march. If not, he then returns to the point where the last spoor was seen. He then moves to the right for about 100m (328ft) before turning back onto the same line of march for about 50–75m (164–246ft). He then turns left again to cross the original line of march, continuing on for about 100m (328ft) before turning right, and then right again to cross the line of march and so on.

360-Degree Search Method

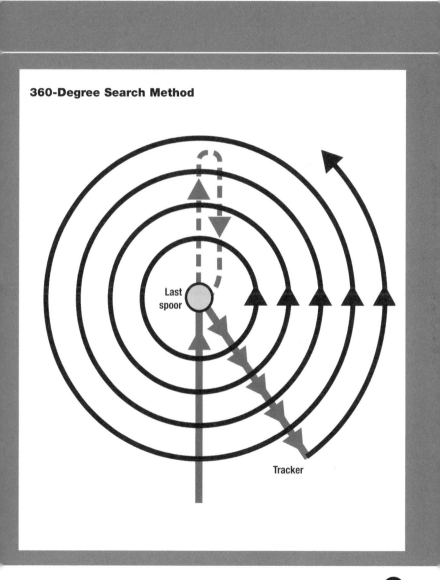

Last spoor

Tracker

Lost Track Drill continued

Box Method

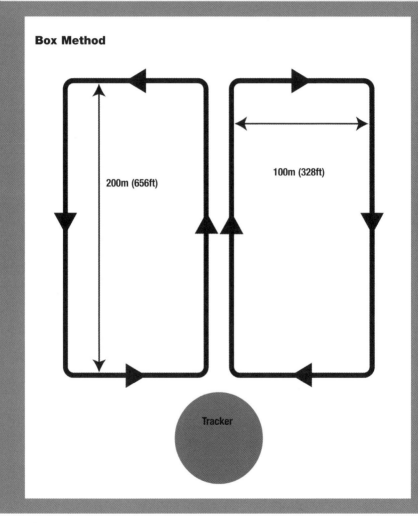

200m (656ft)

100m (328ft)

Tracker

Cross-Grain Search Pattern

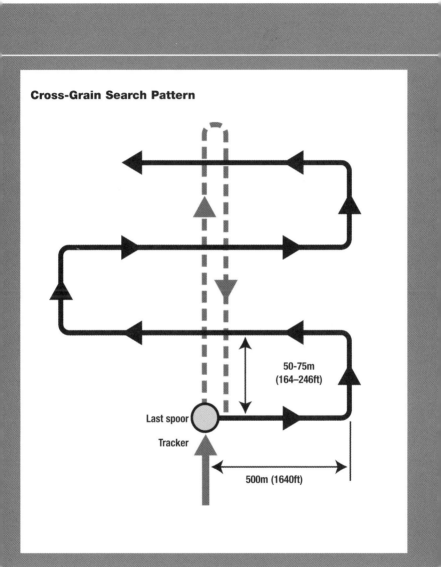

50-75m
(164–246ft)

Last spoor

Tracker

500m (1640ft)

CASE STUDY 3:

Chasing the Balkan War Criminals

After the death of Marshal Tito in 1980, Yugoslavia began to fragment. Slobodan Milošević, head of the league of communists of Serbia, wanted to combine all the Serb elements in a greater Serb republic and used the former Yugoslav National Army (JNA) to enforce his will. The power of Milošević and the JNA was further strengthened by a UN arms embargo against the republics of the former Yugoslavia. When Bosnia-Hercegovina declared independence in 1992, the Bosnian Serbs began to occupy territory and carry out a policy of 'ethnic cleansing'.

As the conflict continued, some of the worst atrocities that Europe had seen since World War II were committed by various parties in the war. In 1993, UN Resolution 827 of the UN Security Council set up the International Criminal Tribunal for the Former Yugoslavia (ICTY), which set about tracking down and bringing to justice the war criminals. Its work continued

after the war was ended at the Dayton Peace Accord on 15 December 1995.

By 2006, over 160 people had been indicted, the most prominent being the former President of Serbia, Slobodan Milošević, who died in his cell before a final judgment was made.

However, many prominent suspected war criminals could not be found, including Radovan Karadžić, former President of Republika Srpska, and Ratko Mladić, the former Bosnian Serb army commander. Others included Simo Drljača, chief of police at Prijedor, Milan Kovačević, President of the Municipal Assembly, and General Stanislav Galić, former commander of the Sarajevo-Romanija Corps of the Army of Republika Srpska (VRS).

These men, and others like them, had all displayed ruthless characteristics and contempt for human life, including genocide, during the war, and were unlikely to give themselves up easily or without a fight. They often also enjoyed the protection of henchmen and were embedded within communities that were suspicious of, if not openly hostile towards, the UN and NATO forces.

Part of the mandate of the new NATO-led stabilization force was to track down those who had been indicted for war crimes. Although this involved the entire force, it was clear that the actual arrests would need to be carried out by highly trained Special Forces, including the British SAS, Dutch 108th Special Operations Company and US Special Forces.

Operation 'Tango'

Although British special operations are not usually officially confirmed, the indications are that a 10-man SAS team was inserted by an RAF Chinook helicopter of 47 Squadron into a remote area of Bosnia-Hercegovina not far from the town of Prijedor, about 113km (70 miles) from the British Sector South-West Headquarters at Banja Luka. The operation involved identifying the two indictees, Simo Drljača and Milan Kovačević, and tailing them until a suitable moment arose for them to be arrested.

As it happened, when Milan Kovačević was approached at the hospital where he worked, he offered no resistance and was led away to a waiting vehicle without incident. Drljača was fishing with his son and brother-in-law, under careful watch by Special Forces located in nearby woods. While the three men were busy making their breakfast, the assault team approached in three cars and a van. Four of the soldiers grabbed the son and brother-in-law while the other six grabbed Drljača himself. At some point, Drljača broke free and fired at one of the soldiers, wounding him in the leg. At this point, the soldiers fired back, killing Drljača instantly.

Arrests were made in a remote area near Prijedor.

Vlatko Kupreškić

As the operation had been largely successful, it was decided to try to apprehend more indictees. This time the target was Vlatko Kupreškić, who had allegedly been involved in a massacre at the village of Ahmici in April 1993.

Kupreškić was likely to be armed and also had a bodyguard. He was observed covertly by a unit of the Dutch 108th Special Forces Company that had been parachuted into an area near Vitez. The Dutch SF team was in liaison with a British SAS team who were waiting to make the arrest.

On Thursday 18 December, the team moved in on the house after dark. The bodyguard was first overcome and then gagged before soldiers entered, having thrown in stun grenades and placed, sentries on the exits. First they secured Kupreškić's wife and children before tackling the man himself. At this point, Kupreškić is said to have fired at the soldiers with a submachine gun. The soldiers were careful when returning fire and hit Kupreškić in the arm and leg, which immobilized him.

General Stanislav Galić

Next on the list was General Stanislav Galić, who had presided over the continuous shelling of Sarajevo as well as the ruthless sniping against civilians. A highway through Sarajevo was even known as 'sniper's alley' and people crossed it at considerable risk of losing their lives. Snipers also fired on people waiting at water stands or for food. Between 1992 and 1994 at least 1399 civilians were killed by snipers and 5093 wounded. The sniping and shelling was under the direct command of General Galić

As a retired general, Galić had considerable influence and many supporters in Banja Luka, where he lived. His supporters and bodyguards were likely to be armed and he was not a man to give up without a fight. The local population could also become hostile and aggressive and cause problems if the arrest were not swift and efficient. After exhaustive surveillance by intelligence assets, an audacious plan was conceived. Despite the dangers, Galić was to be arrested when and where he least expected it – in broad daylight and in a busy street while driving his car.

General Stanislav Galic is arrested by British Special Forces with a mandate from the International Criminal Tribunal for the Former Yugoslavia.

As General Galić left his house on 20 December 1999, an unmarked car and van pulled out incognito behind him and tailed him towards the centre of town. The tailing vehicles contained an SAS snatch squad. The van moved closer to the rear of Galić's car and suddenly the car swept round in front of Galić's car and forced him to stop. Before Galić could reach for his gun, A British soldier had smashed the driver's door window and pulled Galić out onto the road. A sack was immediately placed over his head and his hands cuffed.

Timeline

1993: International Criminal Tribunal for the Former Yugoslavia (ICTY) set up by UN Resolution 827.

10 July 1997: Operation 'Tango' launched, involving SAS teams under command of NATO/SFOR. The targets are Milan Kovačević and Simo Drljača.

18 December 1997: Vlatko Kupreškić is arrested by SAS Special Forces and taken on the same day to the International Criminal Tribunal for the Former Yugoslavia (ICTY).

20 December 1999: General Stanislav Galić is arrested by the SAS in Banja Luka.

21 July 2008: Radovan Karadžić, former President of Republika Srpska, is arrested.

26 May 2011: General Ratko Mladić, former commander of Serb forces, is arrested.

Karadžić and Mladić

The aggressive stance taken by British forces towards indictees meant that 12 out of the 15 arrests were carried out by British forces. However, two of the biggest fish remained at large, namely Radovan Karadžić and General Ratko Mladić, commander-in-chief of Serb forces.

Karadžić was eventually arrested on 21 July 2008, probably because some who knew him decided to go for the considerable reward money. Mladić was arrested on 26 May 2011 by Serbian police officers in the province of Vojvodina. Although he was carrying two pistols, he got no chance to use them.

Mladić was finally arrested in Serbia on 26 May 2011.

The tracking and arrests in Bosnia-Hercegovina were the result of multiple manhunts, involving both high-tech assets as well as intelligence and operational skills on the ground. Once the targets had been identified, arrests had to be carefully planned, as they took place in the midst of potentially hostile local communities, and the targets themselves were often armed and aggressive, often being either former soldiers or police officers. It was one of the greatest mass manhunts of modern history.

U rban tracking presents both the tracker and the quarry with a unique set of challenges that may not be present when tracking in the countryside. Urban areas are largely made up of hard surfaces, so gone are all those obvious footprints in mud, disturbed or marked vegetation, behaviour of wildlife and other clues. In an urban environment, hard asphalt will not hold an obvious footprint and, even if it does, hundreds of other footprints may soon obscure it. In the open country, no other human may be present for miles, whereas in an urban environment the quarry may be simultaneously visible and invisible among the crowds.

Urban Tracking

As urban sprawls have increased worldwide, the art of urban tracking has become ever more important but that does not mean urban tracking is a new phenomenon. In Victorian London, with a population of around seven million, Sir Arthur Conan Doyle created Sherlock Holmes, who habitually followed criminals through the maze of streets with

....

Urban tracking includes a range of techniques such as the art of following without being seen and the use of high-tech devices in a covert way.

3

Urban tracking is a highly sophisticated skill with its own set of unique challenges.

Urban Tracking and Surveillance

their teeming crowds. Sherlock Holmes was an expert tracker and even wrote a monograph on the tracing of footsteps, including methods of preserving footprints in plaster of Paris. Holmes was also a master of observation and deduction, an important part of urban tracking, where physical clues may be few and far between. In *The Sign of Four,* Holmes' faithful companion, Doctor Watson, complements Holmes on his 'extraordinary genius for minutiae', and this highlights another essential characteristic of the urban tracker – that no detail should be overlooked or disregarded.

In the same novel, Holmes and Watson set off on a clattering pursuit in a horse-drawn hansom cab:

I lost my bearings and knew nothing save what seemed to be going a very long way. Sherlock Holmes was never at fault, however, and he muttered the names as the cab rattled through squares and in and out by tortuous by-streets.

Holmes' knowledge of the byways of London was extraordinary, and on this occasion he passed rapidly and with an assured step through a network of mews and stables, the very existence of which I had never known.

This underlines another important aspect of urban tracking and surveillance – an intimate knowledge

Bin Laden latest:

Why does this house have no internet or telephone connections?

of the area in order to successfully plan and carry out the pursuit.

Urban countertracking

As with any form of tracking, it works both ways for both tracker and quarry. If you want to lose yourself in an urban environment and not be noticed, you need to know how to blend in. Move at the same rate as everyone else and look like you have a purpose in mind. If, for example, a tracker is watching a street full of busy people on the way to work, someone loitering and looking directionless is going to stand out from the crowd.

Avoid places where there are 'regulars', such a bars or pubs or even small shops that are likely to have a regular clientele. Keep clean and tidy. Somebody looking unshaven and dishevelled with unbrushed hair may stand out in a street filled with otherwise well-dressed people.

Urban Footprints

Although urban tracking presents unique challenges due to the nature of the environment, it is still possible in some cases to pick up footprints in the traditional way. The dust from these roadworks, for example, means a footprint has been left on the pavement.

Dog Trackers

Dogs are a valuable asset in urban tracking, as they can pick up and follow scents where there is no other evidence of a target having passed that way.

Although the kinds of skills and evidence used in rural tracking are not as viable in an urban environment, it is not necessarily the case that none of these skills can be used. There may, for example, be areas where a road is being dug up and the quarry carries mud or dust of a particular kind on their shoes. Urban areas often have parks and the quarry may leave footprints there.

Use of dogs in urban tracking
Due to the unique challenges of urban tracking, dogs are often used to hunt down fugitives. A dog and tracker team can be a formidable

Counter-Tracking Against Dogs

Running and creating sweat, as well as the sweat produced by fear, provides a stronger scent for a dog to follow and is therefore counter-productive. It is also important to remember that a dog can also easily pick up and distinguish such man-made scents as aftershave, body sprays, hair oil and anything similar, especially if they are not of a type used by the local population.

adversary for an escaping quarry. The dog's unique and powerful sense of smell, as well as its other senses, are allied to the human handler's powers of deduction.

The challenge for dogs in an urban environment is that there is little scent evidence left on hard surfaces, as opposed to the comparatively large amount of scent evidence left by disturbed earth and vegetation. However, the dog can continue to pick up the unique odour of human cells that are shed. In order to pick up those smells, it is best to take dogs out in the early morning, late afternoon or evening. Tracking can also be carried out successfully at night, when there is little air convection. Variations in wind can affect the scent trail for a dog and rain also has an influence on it. There is also a time limit to scent trails, of at most approximately three days. Dogs also have an efficiency limit of about half an hour or so before needing a rest. The handler needs to respect the dog's limitations if he is to get the maximum performance from it.

Crime scene investigation
The starting point for an urban tracking operation can often be a crime scene investigation. Everything that happens during a crime scene investigation is carefully choreographed to minimize the disturbance of any evidence, including the footprints of the quarry.

The first priority of course is the safety and/or recovery of any victims, which overrides every other consideration, including the preservation of evidence. Once that duty has been performed, however, the scene will be cordoned off, allowing only one entrance and exit. Investigators at the scene will wear coveralls and gloves so as not to contaminate the scene with their own hair or clothing. Fingerprints and hand prints may be obvious, and if not obvious they are detected using a dusting technique with fine powder, and then lifted with adhesive tape.

Similarly, any footprints left on hard surfaces will be photographed. If they are left on soft surfaces, they will be set in plaster and taken away for examination. A similar process is also carried out for tyre tracks. This information will then be checked against a computer database to verify the type of shoe or type of tyre, and types of car to which that tyre might be fitted. It may be a tyre usually fitted to high-performance saloon or sports cars of a particular make and model or it may clearly be the tyre print of a sports utility vehicle.

Despite the fact that footprints are a basic key to tracking in rural areas (in fact, the word 'spoor' is the Dutch word for footprint), they are often overlooked in urban areas and crime scenes, coming second to other evidence such as fingerprints. However, footprints can provide a wide range of information about the

Crime Scene

Correct control of a crime scene is crucial for the ongoing success of a manhunt. Evidence must not be disturbed and entry and exit points must be carefully monitored.

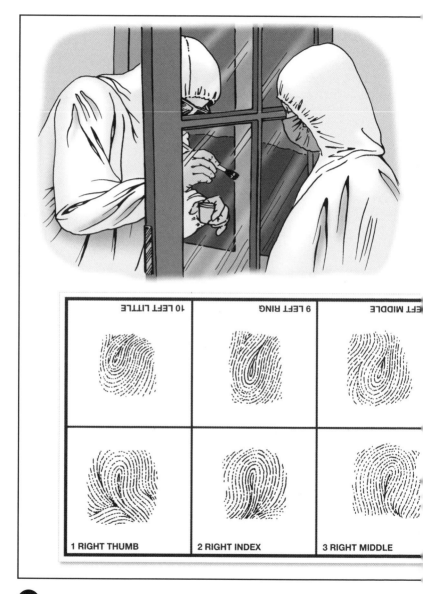

Fingerprinting

Fingerprinting is one of the most useful ways of identifying a suspect, as each person's fingerprint is unique. As ever, it is very important that the crime scene should be undisturbed for this kind of evidence to have maximum benefit.

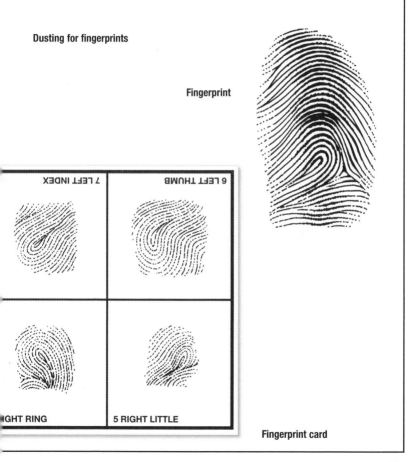

Dusting for fingerprints

Fingerprint

7 LEFT INDEX

6 LEFT THUMB

GHT RING

5 RIGHT LITTLE

Fingerprint card

quarry, including their size, weight, dress code and so on. Furthermore, criminals will often make an attempt to disguise their appearance and wear gloves to prevent fingerprint identification. However, they often make the mistake of paying no attention to their footwear.

When crime scene experts arrive, they will often take great care to isolate and preserve various types of forensic evidence, including fingerprints, but may disregard the fact that they are trampling on important footprint evidence as they come and go. This may also confuse the evidence as to how many people were involved in the crime or incident. Similarly, police, military or other vehicles may obliterate or confuse tyre-print evidence. Entry to and from the area should be performed by a crime-scene officer, who should be aware of the placing of his own footprints, and take care to enter and leave by stepping in his own footprints. The footwear impressions and three-dimensional footprints present at the initial incident site should also be photographed and/or preserved in casts. Their location should be carefully recorded, as this will provide important information as to the direction of travel and the initial important lead required by a tracker.

Footwear impressions on hard surfaces are of course very difficult to find and are mostly invisible to the naked eye. One way to highlight them when indoors can be to darken the room and shine a light on them from an oblique angle. Once discovered, powders used for collecting fingerprints can be used to highlight the shoe print and the pattern can then be picked up using adhesive paper or a similar method. Another method of lifting a footprint is the electrostatic dust lifter, which creates a charge that attracts particles of dust to the lifting film.

Urban Surveillance

Due to the nature of the environment, urban tracking and surveillance are often very complex exercises involving different agents, some of whom will follow a suspect under cover. In order to preserve maximum anonymity, security services often recruit women and people from ethnic minorities who can blend into local communities or appear harmless and inconspicuous. The officers are also required to be highly focused and to be able to track potential criminals and terrorists while remaining unseen or blending into the background.

The problems of remaining incognito in an area where you do not belong can be as difficult for the agent doing the surveillance as for the target. If you sit in a car long enough, waiting for your target to appear, the chances are you will

Making a Footprint Cast

Once a footprint has been identified, a cast is made that can be taken back to the laboratory for further forensic investigation.

Measuring a Footprint Cast

Once a footprint cast has been returned to the laboratory, measurements can be carried out to identify the size of shoe or boot as well as the make and any other identifying factors.

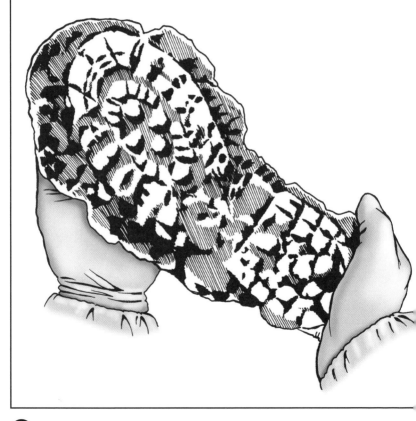

arouse suspicion among local people, who may even call the police, thinking you might be a burglar. One way of reducing suspicion is to have a woman sitting in the passenger seat of the car, who looks like she is waiting for her partner. A woman with a shopping bag in a high street is also unlikely to arouse any suspicion.

Another factor when placing someone under surveillance is that they may move from one environment to another where the clothing and general appearance of everyone is

different. If the suspect moves to a beach area, for example, the tracker may look odd wearing a suit and raincoat. In which case, the tracker may either notify an accomplice who is more suitably dressed or they may carry a change of clothes.

Surveillance skills

A key part of the tracking and manhunt of Osama bin Laden was the successful tracking of his courier, which led surveillance teams to the compound in Abbottabad. Once the compound had been identified as a

Incognito Surveillance

Surveillance can be more difficult than it seems, because someone sitting in a car for long periods can arouse suspicion. Women are less likely to cause concern, especially when sitting in a passenger seat.

Safe House

The CIA Special Activities Division took over a safe house in Abbottabad prior to the raid on Osama bin Laden's compound in 2011. A safe house provides a static place for surveillance from which a picture can be built up of movements to and from a suspect location. The CIA agents would have built a detailed record of what was going on in and around the house, including who visited or left the house and when, and any suspicious activities. They would also have used high-tech visual- and sound-monitoring equipment. The safe house was so

covert that not even Pakistani intelligence knew about it, let alone the occupants of the compound.

In the 1982 Iranian Embassy siege in London, British intelligence units provided a range of monitoring equipment, including microphones in walls and down chimneys, to assess terrorist movements and any threats to the hostages. This was carried out mainly from a safe house next door to the embassy, from where SAS soldiers emerged to place charges at the front of the embassy to force an entrance.

Sheikh Abu Ahmed – the key to finding Osama bin Laden

Abu Ahmed was used as a trusted courier by bin Laden in order to give instructions and other communications to his al-Qaeda subordinates. Al-Qaeda knew that it was impossible to send messages by any other means, whether email or phone, as US intelligence high-tech assets would in due course pick them up and start to trace their origin. The courier was therefore the only link Osama bin Laden had with the outside world, and it was to prove to be a fatal one.

Despite being provided with a nickname for the courier, it took some time to properly identify who it was. Then it took still more time to establish which geographical region he operated in. Once they had identified Abu Ahmed, a full tracking operation was instituted by CIA Special Activities Division Special Operations Groups on the ground.

likely hiding place for Osama bin Laden, CIA operators from the Special Activities Division set up a safe house to monitor activities in the house and around it. Information they provided would have been used to fine-tune the helicopter attack by SEAL Team 6.

The importance of skilled surveillance in a manhunt cannot be overestimated. Although in the modern world a large number of high-tech assets are available to aid surveillance, it also requires a high level of skill to be able to track a suspect on the ground, whether on foot or by car or other means

of transport. For a manhunt to be successful, skilled physical surveillance needs to be combined with high-tech assets in a balanced way but a high level of training in physical surveillance is still required if the operation is to be successful. The other aspect is the level of counter-surveillance that might be expected from particular individuals or organizations. If the target is a small-time criminal, less care needs to be taken in physical surveillance than dealing with a member of a sophisticated organization like al-Qaeda where the target may

Satellites were focused on the area and UAVs and other technological assets brought in. It was crucially important that at no time should the courier be aware that he was being followed, although the combined assets focused on him and the future observation of the compound in Abbottabad would require the CIA to go to the US Congress to ask for further funding for the mission.

Eventually, Abu Ahmed made the move to Abbottabad and a highly sophisticated tailing operation, incorporating some of the methods explained in this chapter, would have taken place, with all his likely exits from his location monitored and perhaps a progressive tailing operation put under way, which would minimize the possibility of him noticing that he was being followed.

be trained in shaking off potential pursuers or who may have a back-up team on the lookout for anybody tailing the target. A properly trained target may decide to engage in a range of surveillance-detection activities to identify any likely pursuers. He may, for example, act in a way that forces the surveillance team to react and then catch them out. However, a well-trained target, such as a professional terrorist, will also be careful to ensure that he does not reveal that he knows that he is under surveillance. He will simply lead his pursuers on a false trail or into a trap or warn other terrorist targets to lie low.

The point at which physical surveillance is activated in a manhunt can depend on a number of factors, but it is usually part of the 'endgame', when enough information has been gathered about a particular target to warrant relatively close physical surveillance. In the case of the manhunt for Osama bin Laden, the links that were made took literally the best part of a decade to construct, feeding off information from interrogations of key suspects, electronic surveillance and so on.

Once the target had been correctly identified, the key was for the tailing team to remain completely invisible, because if Osama bin Laden's trusted courier, Abu Ahmed al-Kuwaiti, had ever had any suspicion that he was being tailed, he would most likely have sounded an alarm or led the tailing team on a wild goose chase. The implications could have been monumental and in theory they could have caused the entire investigation to start again from scratch.

Mobile surveillance

Mobile surveillance, as the name clearly suggests, means surveillance of a target who is in transit from one location to another, either to monitor the target's activities or to provide a lead to a particular destination or link to another target.

The most obvious trap to avoid in mobile surveillance is providing the target with an obvious clue that he is being tailed. This could be a person persistently following him or a particular car always on his tail. To avoid this, mobile surveillance will often be conducted by a team with a form of relay action and it may also involve particular points of static surveillance where the target passes known points and can be watched from a covert position.

It requires a great deal of training and collaboration to manage effective transitions from one surveillance

Mobile Surveillance

Mobile surveillance can be carried out either in vehicles or on foot, or both. It is important never to arouse the suspicions of the target.

operator or team to another. The phases of a surveillance operation are as follows:

- Stakeout: Initially the surveillance team will wait for the target to enter his net of operations. This means establishing a watch over all possible entry and exit points so that the target is not able to pass through unnoticed.
- Pick-Up: The pick-up is the point at which the surveillance team positively identifies the target and signals for the mobile element of the surveillance operation to commence.
- Follow: The follow is the process by which the target is tailed by one or more surveillance operators. The key, as in all parts of a surveillance operation, is to ensure that the target does not notice anything untoward that would alert him to the fact that he is being followed.
- Box: The box phase is where the target stops moving or reaches a particular destination. In the case of the manhunt for Osama bin Laden, this was the phase where the courier reached the compound at Abbottabad. At this point, the pursuit would have stopped and several kinds of surveillance assets concentrated on the area, including satellites. A safe house was also set up at this point to monitor the house.

To some extent, the success or failure of an operation may depend upon the judgment of an individual surveillance operator. This may range from acting in a plausibly inconspicuous manner if the target should turn round and look directly at the operator, to a scenario involving a violent confrontation. Mostly, however, the success of an operator will depend on remaining unnoticed while maintaining the best watch on the target and gathering essential information.

Surveillance operators possess similar qualities to any good tracker or sniper in that they must have the patience to wait, sometimes for long periods with nothing happening, while at the same time maintaining a high level of alertness. They also need to be able to blend in with the surroundings in order to appear inconspicuous. This means adopting ordinary clothing that is suitable for the area or using surveillance operators who are of the same ethnic background as those who live in a particular area. For example, while a tall blonde Westerner will stand out from a crowd of Middle Eastern people of a certain socio-economic group, an operator from that ethnic background will not.

Despite the fact that the operation may involve a considerable level of danger, surveillance operators have to appear unfazed and behave in a manner consistent with the norm of

Surveillance Operator

A surveillance operator has to appear normal and relaxed while being ready to move at a moment's notice. If eating or drinking, it helps to pay the bill beforehand in order to make a swift exit without causing a disturbance.

behaviour around them. For example, if people are dawdling slowly in a busy street, passing the time of day or shopping in a relaxed manner, someone who is obviously nervous or moving rapidly in a focused way will stand out. A surveillance operator may be carrying various pieces of equipment – for example an ear-piece for a communications device – and there could be tell-tale signs that he is using it, such as a hand constantly straying towards the ear.

An operator may also need to adopt a disguise in order to continue a pursuit without being recognized from earlier on, but care should be taken to make the disguise effective and complete, as a trained target will know how to identify certain characteristics about a pursuer that may not have changed despite the disguise, such as wearing the same pair of shoes.

An efficient team of surveillance operators need to be able to dovetail and collaborate seamlessly, often in unfamiliar territory. They need to keep their eyes on the target while simultaneously knowing exactly where they are and passing on accurate information about the whereabouts of the target so that other members of the team can pick up where necessary. What happens if a mobile tailing team get caught in a traffic jam, for example? This is just one of the eventualities that the surveillance operators need to

Blending In

When either conducting surveillance or evading capture, a surveillance operator has to blend in with the surroundings to avoid being noticed. This includes dressing and acting in a way that suits the environment.

Essential Surveillance Equipment

- Binoculars and/or telescope

- Maps

- Global Positioning System

- Compass

- Camera (concealed)

- Torch

- Communications equipment

- Infra-red tracking equipment

- Night-vision device

- Disguise (false beard and so on and change of clothing)

FBI Car Adapted for Surveillance

A surveillance car may be specially fitted with a number of features intended to increase its endurance and enable the surveillance operators to deceive their target.

Controllable brake lights

Reinforced rear bumper

Top-quality shocks

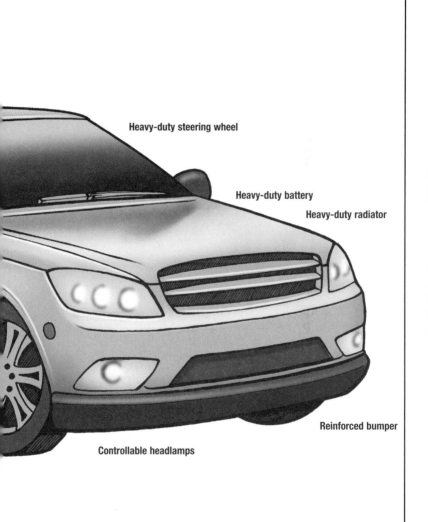

Heavy-duty steering wheel

Heavy-duty battery

Heavy-duty radiator

Reinforced bumper

Controllable headlamps

Hidden Camera

High-tech devices such as a camera hidden in a watch, can provide important information when conducting a surveillance operation.

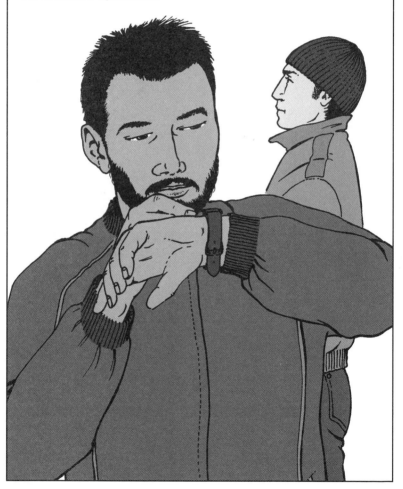

consider when making their pursuit plan. They need to know about the local transport systems so that if the target suddenly gets on a train or bus they know where they are heading. They may need to have bought a travel pass so as to save time buying tickets and so on.

Surveillance vehicles

Surveillance vehicles have to be fully capable of handling any demands that are placed upon them, while also completely inconspicuous. If vehicles in a particular area are generally cheap and ordinary, an expensive SUV will stand out and attract attention. All the details of the surveillance vehicles have to fit in with the other vehicles present, including the number plates.

Whereas in days gone by hidden cameras were the stuff of James Bond movies, now almost everyone with a mobile phone carries a high-specification video camera that can be deployed while attracting very little attention. However, cameras can also be concealed in watches and other pieces of equipment.

The surveillance operators need to compare notes and be absolutely clear about what kind of transport the suspect uses, the number plate of their car and so on, and also be aware that the target might change vehicles during the course of the journey. However, even the best-laid plans can go wrong. In the hunt for

Minimizing Visibility of Surveillance Vehicles

Surveillance vehicles can be fitted with switches that allow the surveillance operator to turn off lights, such as the reversing lights or the brake lights. This allows the surveillance operator to make reversing or braking manoeuvres without attracting undue attention. The number-plate lights can also be extinguished to reduce the likelihood that the target will identify the pursuit car.

However, in traffic it can sometimes be difficult for surveillance cars to recognize each other. One way of getting round this is the system of communicating to the driver of a car ahead to touch the brake pedal so that the red lights flash on momentarily. This needs to be done in a situation where other cars are not braking; otherwise it can be confusing. The request that is given is 'Touch red'.

FBI Tactics for a Stakeout

A stakeout pattern used by security services such as the FBI may involve a box arrangement of vehicles all ready to pick up the tail of the target vehicle, whichever direction it should take. The cheating trigger vehicle pulls in front of the target vehicle to give the signal when the target moves off.

Bravo

Alpha

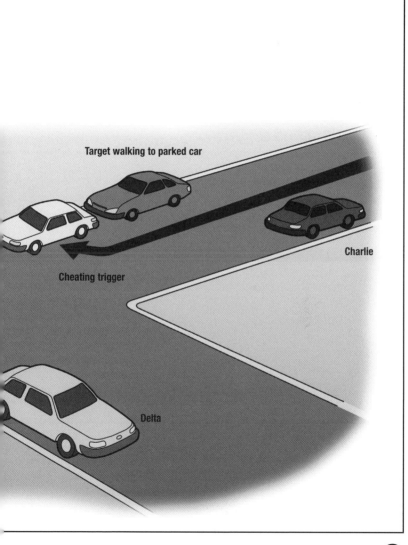

Target walking to parked car

Cheating trigger

Charlie

Delta

Floating Box Technique

The floating-box technique works particularly well in cities where streets and avenues are arranged in a grid pattern. Outside vehicles are ready to pick up the trail if the target should choose to change direction.

Saddam Hussein, for example, a black BMW car was followed until it reached its destination. A black BMW parked outside a house then became the focus of a raid by Special Forces, and the people inside the house were arrested and taken away for interrogation. To the embarrassment of the security forces, however, it turned out to be the wrong black BMW and the people who had been arrested were totally innocent. The real black BMW, which had been the object of the tailing operation, had been parked out of sight in a garage.

In the hunt for the Iraqi terrorist leader Abu Musab al-Zarqawi (see Case Study 5), the cars driven by his spiritual adviser, Sheikh Abu Abd al Rahman, became the key to the endgame. Interrogation had revealed that if at any point al Rahman switched cars from a white saloon to a blue saloon this meant that he was on his way to visit al-Zarqawi. Although from the target's perspective the switch of cars was no doubt intended to confuse any potential pursuers, in reality it simply confirmed his intentions. Without the advantage of prior intelligence, however, the switch of cars may have thrown off the pursuers if it had been managed skilfully.

A team of operators may cover a target vehicle with a number of vehicles in order to cover all eventualities. In a city with a grid system of roads, for example, the

Blind Corners

Blind corners can be useful for maintaining a covert presence but the target can sometimes turn the tables on a pursuer by turning a blind corner and waiting. If this happens, the pursuer needs to continue as if nothing was amiss.

Brevity Codes used in the UK by units such as Special Branch

Brevity codes are often used by surveillance personnel as a message shorthand to cut down the amount of time on the radio. It means a situation can be conveyed and understood with the use of only one or two words. Different brevity codes are used by different organizations, and all members of an operation need to be fully briefed on the relevant codes.

HA | Home address

TA | Target address

OP | Observation point (private dwelling or empty flat etc)

CPS | Central police station

RECIPROCAL | Target returning on same route

NATURAL | The call of nature (loo)

MOODY | Target looking around, showing excess caution etc

TK | Telephone kiosk

YES YES | Correct radio procedure for 'yes'

NO NO | Correct radio procedure for 'no'

SO FAR | Last transmission received

GO | Unit has permission to transmit

STRIKE | Command by senior official for strike on premises or target

FRIENDLIES | Plainclothes policeman mingling with suspects

NO CHANGE | Current situation is unaltered

PERMISSION | Unit asking for permission to transmit message

TARGET | Subject or premises under observation

DRUM | Target's dwelling

THE FACTORY | Refers to CPS or units main office

STOP STOP | Target has stopped (a warning to approaching units)

COVERT | Sun visor or body-worn disguised microphone

ORIGINAL | Target resumed heading in original direction

WAIT ONE | Unit told to hold next transmission

PNC | Police National Computer (vehicle checks)

EYEBALL | Covert officer with closest visual on target

CONTACT | Target or target's vehicle relocated after search

CONVOY | Series of vehicles following target also in vehicle

Brevity Codes continued

NOT EQUIPPED | Usually means that a unit has no force-wide VHF radio

NOTED | Transmission received and understood

FOOT MAN | Officer on foot, usually in the immediate area of the target

BATPHONE | Unofficial word for h/held Motorola 8000S cellular phone

WOODENTOP | Unofficial word for uniformed police officer

LOG | Refers to log kept of all target movements

BIG AIR | Refers to unit monitoring regular police channels

SCOPE | Refers to a night-vision device (image intensifier)

STAND DOWN | Order to conclude that day's operation

OFF OFF | Target in on the move (some units say 'lift-off')

NO DEVIATION | Target continuing in original direction

surveillance operating team may both track the target vehicle visually as well as travelling on parallel roads so that the target will remain covered in the event of making a sudden turn. The technique whereby a target is kept within a box in this way, with tracking vehicles on parallel roads on each side, is called a floating box.

For the floating box to work, there have to be constant communications between the members of the pursuit team so that if one car gets caught in traffic, others can take over.

BAULKED | Target or unit is held by lights or heavy traffic

2 UP ETC | Identifies number of people in vehicle

BURNED | Unit car or officer is believed to have been spotted

BLOW OUT | Target is believed to be aware of surveillance

BACK-UP | Unit behind eyeball vehicle waiting to take the lead

TWO CLICKS | Covert way of using h/held PTT button to answer no

THREE CLICKS | Covert way to answer 'yes'/or indicate last message received

Nothing heard indicates that no response was received over the radio

As in yes-yes and no-no, many of the previous brevity codes are repeated two or three times to ensure correct reception by other units.

Foot surveillance

In addition to all the precautions the surveillance operator should take with regard to dress, conforming to the ethnic and social norm and so on, the operator has constantly to be aware of the importance of not acting or reacting in a way that will attract the attention of a suspicious target who may suddenly turn round and look at them. Peeking from behind a newspaper or from a doorway is bound to attract attention. If the surveillance operator suddenly stops

Following a Suspect onto Public Transport

On public transport, the key for a surveillance operator is to maintain visual contact without appearing suspicious.

or moves quickly into cover when the target turns round this is likely to confirm the target's suspicions. In these circumstances, the surveillance operator has to behave as if oblivious to the target. If the target remains motionless, the operator must continue walking casually, straight past the target.

The box method, in which a number of surveillance operators are keeping an eye on a target, may mean that operators have to wait in shops or restaurants while the target approaches. However, they need to make sure that they do not wait so long as to arouse suspicion. A surveillance operator sitting in a restaurant will naturally be expected to order something to eat. So it is essential to be able to finish the meal and pay for it quickly if the target passes by.

Surveillance operators need to be aware of a tactic sometimes used by suspicious targets as a means of counter-surveillance, whereby the target goes round a blind corner by a building and stops to see who follows them. An inexperienced surveillance operator may appear startled as he follows round and bumps into the target. This may prove to be a give-away unless the operator is very good at maintaining composure. In order to prevent this happening, surveillance operators are taught to walk past a blind corner, checking with their peripheral vision

Keeping the Suspect in Sight

Although the target must be kept in sight, it is important not to catch his eye or do anything to trigger suspicion. Do not hold up a newspaper without reading it properly, for example.

that the target has walked on and signalling to a follow-on operators that they should pick up the chase.

Surveillance on public transport

Following a target on public transport can be complicated for all sorts of reasons, one of which is knowing the target's destination. The surveillance operator needs either to get close enough to the target to hear what ticket he asks for when buying it; or operators can buy a network ticket to cover most destinations, if that is available. It also helps to know the destination, so that vehicles and teams can be despatched to pick up the trail on the target at the destination.

Depending on how many operators are in the surveillance team, and what the arrangements are for follow-on at the destination, one or more of the surveillance team will need to board the train with the target. When on the train, if one surveillance operator gets close to the target in order to monitor his movements, his position will be compromised for future operations, as he is likely to be recognized by the target.

When the target gets off the train, the surveillance operators need to ensure that the target does not see them, if they are not to be compromised when continuing the follow. As it is likely that the target may pick up a taxi, surveillance vehicles already on the spot need to conduct a follow-on operation.

Follow-on Operation

In surveillance operations involving public transport, sometimes it is possible to arrange for part of the surveillance team to be waiting at the platform to pick up the trail.

CASE STUDY 4:
The Quest for Saddam Hussein

After a frustrating series of negotiations and interventions by UN weapons inspectors in Iraq, the United States and Britain decided to cease diplomatic processes with Iraq by the end of 2002. On 17 March 2003, President George W. Bush gave Saddam Hussein an ultimatum to leave Iraq or face war. The United States and Britain had made detailed preparations for an invasion, the Americans aiming for Baghdad, while the British aimed for the southern part of Basra. The Coalition forces began their attacks on 20 March 2003.

By 9 April, Baghdad had fallen to US forces and Saddam Hussein went into hiding, having survived an initial attempt to kill him with Tomahawk cruise missiles. The Coalition forces, after their convincing conventional military defeat of Iraqi force, now faced two problems: a growing insurgency and the fact that the figurehead of the Ba'ath regime was still at large. A massive manhunt therefore ensued.

Task Force 20

Task Force 20 was the special operations group assigned to track down Saddam Hussein and his coterie. A highly select undercover detachment was in Baghdad before the formal commencement of hostilities to try to direct aircraft attacks on to a bunker where Saddam Hussein was believed to be hiding. An F117/A Nighthawk duly dropped a 907kg (2,000lb) bomb on to the house of a Ba'ath Party general but, as it

Saddam Hussein was found in Ad-Dawr in Tikritt, Iraq.

later transpired, Saddam was not there at the time. The immediate problem was that nobody knew where he was or whether he had in fact been killed. It was unlikely that there would be any evidence after such a large bomb.

On 22 July 2003, an operation began to flush out Saddam's sons, Uday and Qusay, from a large house in the Falah district of Mosul. Task Force 20 were given the assignment, supported by 2nd Brigade of 101st Division. The assault force ran into fire from the building and the attack was called off. Despite the fact that the building received 12.7mm (0.5in) machine-gun and rocket fire from the support forces, resistance continued. Eventually the occupants of the house were killed by anti-tank missiles.

Sergeant Eric Maddox

Sergeant Eric Maddox, an interrogator for the US Defence Intelligence Agency, has been credited with the major intelligence breakthrough that resulted in the discovery and capture of Saddam Hussein. Soon after Sergeant Maddox arrived in Baghdad, he found himself accompanying a hit squad whose mission was to find insurgents and high-value targets.

These included a group of loyal bodyguards who were often related in some way to Saddam Hussein. There was also an elite Black List of highly wanted suspects, with Saddam Hussein at the top of the list, 'Chemical Ali' at number five and Izzat Ibrahim Al-Duri at number six. For Eric Maddox, driving through the streets of Baghdad at high speed and then raiding a house potentially full of insurgents was not too much of a shock, as he had once been a US Ranger. However, a friendly-fire incident involving a 12.7mm (0.5in) machine-gun certainly focused his mind.

In preliminary interviews, Sergeant Maddox began to probe low-ranking bodyguards who inadvertently gave away useful information during the course of conversation, proving that although the human mind is very agile, it is still difficult to monitor and sieve everything you say during the course of fast repartee, especially when tired and demoralized by capture. Eric Maddox knew that now that Saddam Hussein had disappeared, his ex-henchmen had to trade off their traditional fear of their ex-President against the new reality of the US invasion and the likelihood of being locked up and

Found Underground

Skilful interrogation techniques eventually pinpointed a farmhouse in Tikrit, where Saddam Hussein was found in a hiding hole.

Timeline

20 March 2003: Invasion of Iraq by US and UK forces begins.

6 April 2003: British forces enter Basra.

9 April 2003: Baghdad conquered by US forces.

22 July 2003: Operation to capture Uday and Qusay Hussein results in both of their deaths.

12 December 2003: raid on a house in Tikrit results in the capture of Muhammad Ibrahim, Saddam Hussein's right-hand man and the one who knew the exact location where Saddam Hussein was hiding.

13 December 2003: Saddam Hussein located by US Special Forces and G Troop, 10th Cavalry.

2005–06: Saddam Hussein appears before Iraq's Special Tribunal to answer charges of crimes against humanity.

5 November 2006: Saddam Hussein is found guilty and is sentenced to death by hanging

30 December 2006: Saddam Hussein hanged.

The manhunt was over.

someone throwing away the key. The human instinct for self-preservation is a strong one and Maddox knew that this was one game of cards in which he needed to play his hand carefully.

Not only does an interrogator need to be a good card player, he also needs to be a good actor. Getting angry at the right time or knowing when to be friendly are key elements in this job. Just as actors are often born not made, skilled interrogators have the right instincts about when to strike and when to hold back. Maddox had a natural ability to form a picture in his mind based on information given to him and he could also accurately identify bits that did not fit the picture.

Saddam located

The hunt for Saddam Hussein continued with a series of raids looking for key supporters who might provide essential leads. A raid by 720th Military Police, for example, led to the capture of a key lead. One thing led to another, and a raid took place on 13 November in Tikrit that yielded more useful informants.

As more candidates came in for questioning, Maddox began to build a three-dimensional picture. Questions to different people helped to confirm or deny previous lists of information. Sometimes, the information was apparently innocuous detail, such as Saddam Hussein's favourite food. However, Maddox kept a log of all the details, just in case.

The interview of a driver ostensibly now helping the Americans yielded little information to start with until Maddox arranged for him to be placed under arrest. At this point the rules of the game changed and Maddox had some leverage. The information subsequently revealed allowed Maddox to get inside the inner workings of the insurgency leadership structure at the highest level. The next target was Muhammad Ibrahim, head of insurgency operations in Iraq and reporting to only one person – Saddam Hussein. The nature of modern insurgency is such that its headquarters was a cement store. The key interviewees in the final run-up to the capture of Saddam Hussein proved to be a couple of innocent-looking fishermen.

Soon Maddox found himself briefing the commander of the task force in Iraq, Admiral William McRaven, future head of US Special Operations Command. Maddox was running out of time, as he was due to be redeployed back to the United States.

Saddam's Hideout

The compound where Saddam Hussein was hiding included a farmhouse and a hole under the ground with a Styrofoam cover and a ventilation shaft.

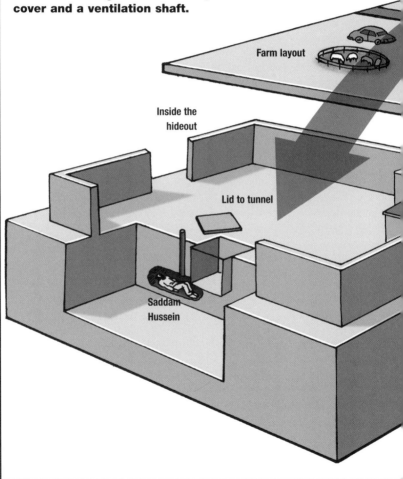

Farm layout

Inside the hideout

Lid to tunnel

Saddam Hussein

Hideout

Fortunately for him, however, the hit team had also done some fishing and came back with a big catch – Muhammad Ibrahim himself. It was only a matter of time before Ibrahim realized which side his bread was buttered on and that he and his family would be in a far better position if he led the Americans to the place where Saddam Hussein was hiding.

On 13 December the chase unit was told to move to east Tikrit. The operation included Special Forces and G Troop, 10th Cavalry. In a farmhouse courtyard, Saddam Hussein was finally found, hiding ignominiously in a hole.

A modern manhunt may cross national borders and will require the deployment of a range of high-technology assets on the ground, in the air and in space to maximize information-gathering potential for both the actual target and any known associates.

Visual Surveillance

Visual surveillance can be carried out by police, intelligence units and security forces on the ground using powerful telescopes, binoculars, telephoto lens cameras and closed-circuit television (CCTV). Units working under cover of darkness can use passive thermal-imaging devices that allow them to see in the dark. Users of mobile phones are familiar with small cameras that once were only available to secret agents, and these can, of course, be used easily by operatives on the ground, without arousing any great suspicion. Surveillance cameras can also be hidden in watches and pens for totally covert use.

Audio surveillance systems include an array of covert microphones and radio transmitters. A self-contained

. . . .

High-tech assets typically deployed in a modern manhunt often include unmanned aerial vehicles (UAVs), asymmetric computer assets and thermal imaging equipment.

4

Technological assets play a vital role in a manhunt in the modern era and encompass a wide range of tools.

High Tech

Police CCTV footage

Information from closed-circuit television cameras (CCTV) can be used to identify suspicious behaviour and potential terrorist activity.

Thermal imaging

Thermal imaging equipment comes in many forms and can be used by both military and civilian personnel to track suspects at night.

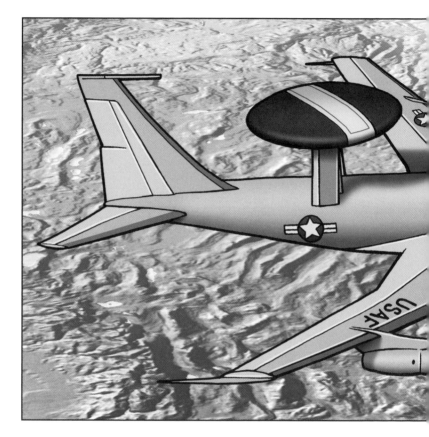

wireless microphone may be a very tiny object that can be hidden just about anywhere.

Aerial Surveillance

Conventional modern aircraft of various types carry sophisticated monitoring equipment for intelligence-gathering. The British Royal Air Force, for example, deploys a modified Beechcraft King Air 350CER with an L-3 Wescam MX-15 electro-optical/infrared camera as well as an array of other sensor equipment. Battlefield and other ground surveillance systems are also covered in a modified Bombardier Global Express aircraft, operated by No.5 (AC) Squadron. The RAF also deploy Britten Norman

E-3 Sentry

Airborne surveillance such as the Airborne Warning and Control System (AWACS) can provide battlefield mastery as well as information on terrorist and insurgency movements.

U.S. AIR FORCE

Islander aircraft from RAF Northolt to carry out surveillance such as the monitoring of phone communications between suspects.

US aerial surveillance includes the E8 Joint Surveillance Target Attack Radar System (Joint STARS), mounted in an adapted Boeing 707 with modern Pratt & Whitney engines. Although the system is primarily

designed for battlefield surveillance and management and for detecting the advance of enemy armour, it is also capable of tracking personnel, such as groups of Taliban fighters in the Afghanistan operational area.

Perhaps the best-known airborne warning and control system (AWACS) is the Boeing E-3 Sentry, also based on the Boeing 707 platform. The E-3

UAV

UAVs such as the RQ-1A Predator provide both surveillance and forward observation capabilities as well as target engagement when required.

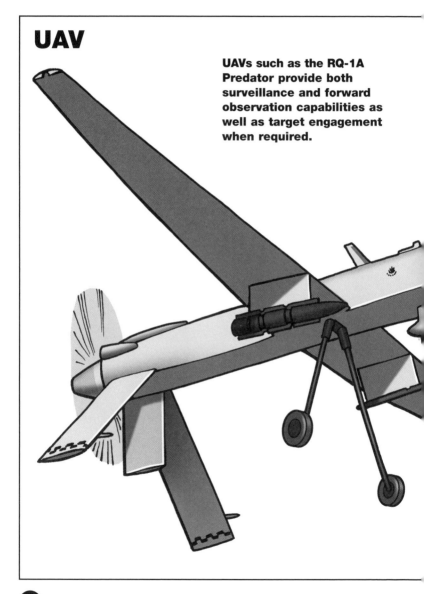

Bin Laden latest:

In Abbottabad, false walls and entrances on the house are discovered.

is capable of providing air and ground battlefield control as well as early warning at considerable distances. For example, US and British Special Forces on the ground in Iraq during Operation 'Desert Storm' would probably have had their communications with attack aircraft routed through E-3 Sentry AWACS.

Unmanned aerial vehicles

Aerial surveillance has become more and more important with the increased use of unmanned aerial vehicles (UAVs) as well as a range of manned surveillance aircraft and helicopters.

Alongside the advance in UAV technology comes an advance in camera technology with hawk-like focus capable of identifying small objects from an altitude of 18,288m (60,000ft). They can also carry infra-red devices that can identify human body heat about 60km (37 miles) away. Micro Air Vehicles (MAVs) are

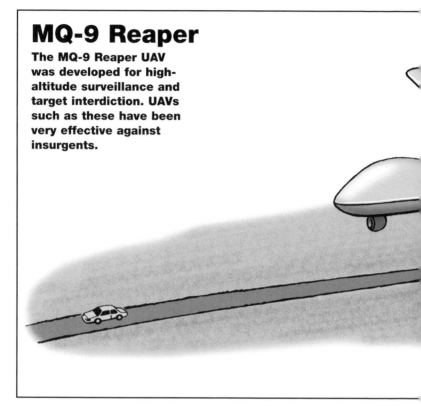

MQ-9 Reaper

The MQ-9 Reaper UAV was developed for high-altitude surveillance and target interdiction. UAVs such as these have been very effective against insurgents.

under development which can carry very small cameras and operate inside buildings. Future plans include MAVs the size of insects that can mimic flapping flight.

Drones or UAVs have been used in various forms for many years, including World Wars I and II and in the Vietnam War, where 100th Strategic Reconnaissance Wing flew several thousand missions. Although the attrition rate was high, to some extent this did not matter as there was no pilot on board and therefore the only real loss was the cost of the equipment. The same remains true today. As aerial reconnaissance can be a hazardous business, since it involves hanging around for a certain amount of time over enemy territory and, in particular, in sensitive areas where an enemy is

likely to field anti-aircraft defences, whether guns or missiles, the advantages of having a pilotless aircraft are obvious.

Within the US armed forces, UAVs are designated according to their flight levels and capabilities in so-called tiers. The first tier incorporates a remote controlled UAV not unlike the remote-controlled aircraft flown by enthusiasts in parks

and elsewhere. Fitted with a high-resolution camera, this aircraft can provide situation awareness without risk to its controllers. It can also function autonomously.

A more formidable UAV operating at higher altitude is the MQ-9 Reaper. This is operated by both the USAF and RAF as well as the US Navy and the Italian air force. The Reaper has extreme potential for reconnaissance of suspects and targets such as individual or groups or terrorists. It is estimated, for example, that the Reaper's camera can read a vehicle number plate from a distance of 3.2km (2 miles). Should the suspects be positively identified as enemies posing a direct threat, the Reaper has a formidable array of weaponry to neutralize a wide range of targets. Weapons include GBU-12 Paveway II laser-guided bombs, AGM-114 Hellfire air-to-ground missiles, and AIM-9 Sidewinder and AIM-92 Stinger air-to-air missiles. Reapers are already used, not only in Afghanistan where they had combat duties at the time of writing, but also for border patrols in mainland north America under control of the US Department of Homeland Security.

The Royal Air Force also operates Reapers (known as a Remotely Piloted Air System [RPAS]) in Afghanistan against Taliban insurgents. It is designated by the RAF as primarily an intelligence, surveillance and reconnaissance (ISR) asset, although it is also designated for close air support (CAS) operations when necessary. The success of initial deployments meant that the RAF was soon doubling its order for the aircraft.

Moving up the size and capability scale is the Northrop Grumman RQ-4 Global Hawk, which has high-altitude capabilities and is fitted with Synthetic Aperture Radar that can penetrate cloud cover and a range of other surveillance capabilities, including electro-optical devices and infrared sensors.

Satellite surveillance

The latest developments in satellite surveillance, and particularly in military satellite technology, mean that satellites in space can now provide real-time video coverage of people on the ground at very high resolutions. The technology also allows for identification of chemicals and other substances. Satellites can collect images as well as a range of signals and communications intelligence.

Signals Intelligence (SIGINT)

The interception of signals has for a long time been a vital way of tracking down individuals or discovering what an enemy's strategy might be in wartime. Signals or communications might be intercepted, and then code-breakers may have to work out what the signals mean if they are encrypted. Signals intercepts in World War II and their decoding as part of the ULTRA programme were a key factor in many successful Allied operations.

Intercepting command signals sent out by major national armed forces in major conflicts is one thing; however, dealing with the more random and sporadic communications of terrorists

Satellite Surveillance

Satellite surveillance proved crucial in the hunt for Osama bin Laden. Some satellites can be manoeuvred in space so as to pinpoint the locations of phone calls.

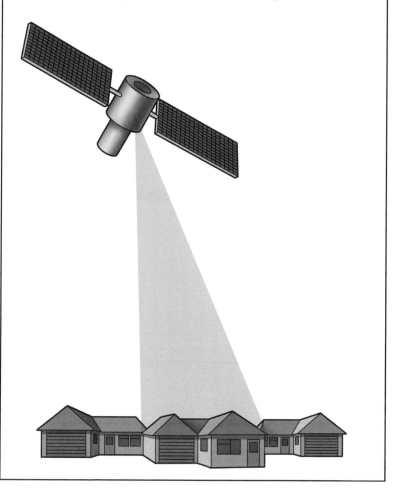

Sidewinder Missile

The AIM-9 Sidewinder missile is carried by UAVs such as the MQ-9 Reaper and can be used against terrorist and insurgent targets

CIA Special Activities Division/Special Operations Groups UAV strikes

Unmanned aerial vehicles (UAVs) have been used with considerable effectiveness by CIA Special Activities Division/Special Operations Groups in Afghanistan and other places.

On 14 February 2008, 27 Taliban and al-Qaeda fighters were killed by a missile fired from a drone in south Waziristan. This was only one of a number of incidents where covert CIA teams used drones to kill dozens of insurgents. It was estimated that, in May 2009 alone, about 50 al-Qaeda fighters were killed by drones, showing the effectiveness of UAVs used in a covert context. Soon, the number of Taliban and al-Qaeda fighters killed by drones was numbered in hundreds, and the US Government commented on the outstanding success of the programme and provided further investment.

The UAVs used by CIA SAD/SOG units were MQ-1 Predator and MQ-9 Reaper. The Predator is armed with Hellfire missiles, capable of destroying a tank. The Reaper can carry 230kg (500lb) bombs as well as Hellfires.

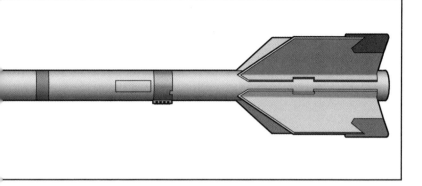

in the modern era is something else altogether. However, although terrorists may not be operating in quite the same way as formal military groups, the sophistication of signals communications for organizations such as al-Qaeda should never be underestimated.

Carrying out major international terrorist attacks such as the attack on the World Trade Center in New York in September 2001, the Madrid train bombings in March 2004 and the London Transport bombings in July 2005, and to achieve all of this, without being spotted by either national or international intelligence organizations, required a highly sophisticated network of communications. Al-Qaeda, for example, ran numerous safe houses in the Middle East, Europe and North America, and maintained its communications network through highly sophisticated computer

hardware that included the ability to track US intelligence satellites. Al-Qaeda also had the ability to send encrypted information around the world without detection. Terrorist organizations such as these are often able to draw on the expertise of disenchanted intelligence professionals who bring with them a wealth of knowledge about how to carry out both intelligence and counter-intelligence operations.

The advantage of such highly organized terrorist groups have over large national intelligence services is that they are usually small scale, sophisticated and highly mobile. In order to respond in kind, national and international organizations have had to develop more flexible and adaptive intelligence-gathering systems that combine a range of intelligence-gathering options, including high-tech assets in space, in the air and on the ground, as well as human intelligence (HUMINT), gathered through agents on the ground and other specialists.

United States Intelligence Services

In the United States, the bulk of intelligence is handled by the Central Intelligence Agency (CIA), but US military forces retain their own separate intelligence assets and there is also the Defence Intelligence Agency (DIA), State Department Intelligence and the Federal Bureau of Investigation (FBI). All of these report to the National Security Agency (NSA). After the attacks on the World Trade Center in September 2001, the US Government created the Department of Homeland Security, which included intelligence analysts from the CIA. Because of some controversy after the September 2001 attacks over the sharing of information between separate intelligence organizations, such as the CIA and FBI, CIA intelligence officers are now assigned to FBI units and vice versa. This is designed to prevent any vital information falling between two stools.

The CIA has increased its ability to provide active intelligence on the ground, whether on the battlefield or in operations against terrorists, while the FBI deals with domestic counter-intelligence and counter-terrorism in co-ordination with the

Global Surveillance

Satellite surveillance is a global operation involving receivers and information centres in many Allied countries.

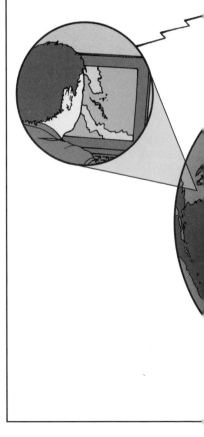

Reporting Back

Intelligence agents monitor the situation in the countries where they are posted and report their findings back to HQ.

CIA. The NSA is responsible for signals intelligence, including the interception of any kind of signal or message worldwide and its analysis or, where necessary, decryption. The message interception includes any form of commercial email or phone message that might be regarded as suspicious. The Echelon programme is run in conjunction with Canada, the United Kingdom, Australia and New Zealand. Although originally designed to counter the intelligence activities of the Soviet Union and its allies, a large proportion of Echelon activities are now probably focused on intercepts between terrorist organizations and cells. Intercepts are largely focused on satellite telecommunications, and a new challenge for intelligence interception has been the increased use of fibre-optic cables for telecommunications.

The US National Reconnaissance Office deploys and controls US intelligence-gathering satellites. The satellites are typically delivered into space on Atlas V rockets and a typical payload could be either a signals, imagery or communications satellite. Latest developments have included small satellites that are easier to deploy and which have the potential for being used in formations to acquire intelligence. Signals intelligence satellites were used for identifying phone calls made by aides of Osama bin Laden and to use the signals as a means of pinpointing the geographical location of the caller.

United Kingdom Intelligence Services

Signals intelligence in England stretches all the way back to the 16th century when Queen Elizabeth I's spymaster, Sir Francis Walsingham, was intercepting mail packages between suspects. Modern incarnations of the intelligence services are usually known as MI5 and MI6 (the designation coming from Military Intelligence room 5 or 6), known for their important roles in World War II. Their civilian names are the Secret Intelligence Service (MI6) and the British Security Service (MI5).

Both of these services are actively involved in 'manhunts' for suspected terrorists. For MI5, however, the emphasis, although not exclusively so, is on home territory; meanwhile, for MI6 the focus is on intelligence-gathering and operations abroad. MI6 agents would typically be involved in the manhunt for Osama bin Laden, Colonel Gaddafi or any other similar high-value targets. The more active side of operations would be likely to be conducted by Special Forces, although some MI6 officers are themselves recruited from the Special Forces and therefore possess a high level of arms training.

CIA Special Activities Division

The United States Central Intelligence Agency (CIA) incorporates a National Clandestine Service of which the Special Activities Division (SAD) is a section. The SAD is divided into two parts – one for covert political action and the other for paramilitary special operations. The Political Action Group within the SAD covers a range of influences, including psychological, economic, political and cyber.

The paramilitary operations are carried out by the Special Operations Group (SOG) incorporated within SAD. The primary mission for the SOG is gathering intelligence in hostile territories in a covert manner and influencing events without overt involvement from the US Government. Operatives with SOG would not be readily identified as US personnel. Typical involvement for such paramilitaries would be assistance in hunting down high-value targets. SOG operators were responsible for the tracking of Osama bin-Laden's courier to the Abbottabad compound, after which they set up a CIA safe house that provided information for the planning of the SEAL Team 6 attack.

SAD and SOG operatives carry on operations in 'denied' areas and have been responsible for capturing a large number of key al-Qaeda operators. SAD/SOG paramilitary forces operated with considerable success in Afghanistan, where they set up and ran Counter-terrorism Pursuit Teams (CTPT). By 2010 there were about 3,000 operators in these teams and they were deployed in both known conventional combat areas as well as remote tribal areas where there was no other official government or military force present. The units also operated across the border with Afghanistan, where they targeted al-Qaeda and Taliban personnel.

US Intelligence Badges

US intelligence agencies cover the spectrum of both civilian and defence, home and international intelligence-gathering and interception. Collaboration between the agencies has been increased in the wake of the 9/11 attacks in New York and Washington.

MI5 Badge

UK intelligence agencies include the home service (MI5), foreign service (MI6) and the British Defence Intelligence Service. They are all controlled by the Joint Intelligence Committee.

Typically, MI5 or MI6 officers provide the communications intelligence-gathering equipment and expertise, although the boundary between civilian intelligence officers and active special operations soldiers has largely been bridged by the creation of the relatively new Special Reconnaissance Regiment. In civilian operations, intelligence officers will provide necessary leads to suspects but, under British law, they cannot themselves make an arrest. It is therefore up to a police unit such as Special Branch to make the case for the arrest. When brought to court, some suspects walk free due to human rights legislation allowing defence lawyers to demand explicit information from intelligence services as to how they identified and tracked the suspect. As it would be a breach of national security to divulge such information, the case cannot therefore proceed. The British Defence Intelligence Service is the joint arm of the three British armed services – navy, army and air force. The Joint Intelligence Committee (JIC) oversees all British intelligence services' activities.

Human Intelligence

Despite the wide array of high-tech assets, human intelligence (HUMINT) remains a valuable and even vital part of the intelligence required to conduct an efficient manhunt. The way this intelligence is gathered

The Hunt for Colonel Gaddafi

At the time of writing, an example of the co-ordination between British MI6 agents and British Special Forces came up in the search for the recently deposed dictator of Libya, Colonel Gaddafi. Reports stated that 22 SAS Regiment were in Libya, where they would be providing fire-control for RAF aircraft and also ready to pounce on Gaddafi and his henchmen. Meanwhile, MI6 and CIA officers were using contacts on the ground to try to find a trail to the deposed leader. From Britain, the government eavesdropping centre at Cheltenham (GCHQ) worked hard to intercept communications using a range of technology. This included the ability to match Gaddafi's voice on any calls he made using a satellite telephone. Intelligence would also have been gathered and shared through US technological and HUMINT assets.

Human Intelligence

Intelligence operators have to pass through rigorous training before being eligible to take up a post in the highly complex world of intelligence.

Communicating with Locals

Fostering good relations with local communities has benefits all round and can lead to useful intelligence information.

varies across a wide spectrum of contacts and human relations to hands-on interrogation and sometimes coercion.

Getting the inside track and building up an array of contacts is partly the field of diplomatic relations and sometimes diplomats act as intelligence officers. Information can be gathered from diplomats in formal and informal meetings, the work of military attachés, non-governmental staff who work for charities, refugees, journalists, travellers, espionage and covert surveillance by Special Forces.

Making Judgments

There is always, however, the possibility that information gathered may be too random or may have been deliberately provided in order to deceive. Intelligence officers have to make judgments about whether their sources are trustworthy, lest they find themselves drawn into a trap or place others in danger. One way of judging the value of a particular piece of information or a lead is to get more than one unrelated source to confirm the information. Senior officers have to make the decision whether leads that have been gathered from the 'front line' should be followed. The intelligence assessment that is made may contain a range of information of varying value, some of which may be incorrect or provided in order to mislead.

Part of understanding how people and systems work in a particular country is to understand its culture. Intelligence officers and sometimes Special Forces will learn the language of the country they are visiting and learn about its culture. Having a knowledge of the language and culture has its advantages: it allows the intelligence officer a greater range of contacts; and it enables the intelligence officer to judge how people are likely to behave in given situations and how they are likely to react.

The 'hearts and minds' approach taken by British Special Forces during the Malayan Emergency in the 1960s allowed the soldiers to create valuable alliances among the local population and to be able to take advantage of their considerable skills, such as tracking. Positive relations between the soldiers and local villagers made it less likely that the villagers would harbour terrorists and more likely that they would pass on valuable information about their activities. Similarly, T.E. Lawrence, when organizing the Arab Revolt during World War 1, was from the outset determined to understand the ways of the Arabs and to live as they did. He dressed as they did, ate as they did and copied and sometimes exceeded their feats of exceptional physical endurance in vast desert areas. In this way he earned their trust and respect. The other side of the coin is that

Diplomatic Relations

Military personnel are often involved in humanitarian work, providing essential supplies for communities in need and mending roads and bridges.

Interrogation

Special Forces and other military and intelligence personnel at high risk of capture are trained in resistance to interrogation.

Articles of the Third Geneva Convention Relevant to Prisoners and Interrogation

ARTICLE 13

Prisoners of war must at all times be humanely treated. Any unlawful act or omission by the Detaining Power causing death or seriously endangering the health of a prisoner of war in its custody is prohibited, and will be regarded as a serious breach of the present Convention. In particular, no prisoner of war may be subjected to physical mutilation or to medical or scientific experiments of any kind which are not justified by the medical, dental or hospital treatment of the prisoner concerned and carried out in his interest. Likewise, prisoners of war must at all times be protected, particularly against acts of violence or intimidation and against insults and public curiosity.

Measures of reprisal against prisoners of war are prohibited.

ARTICLE 14

Prisoners of war are entitled in all circumstances to respect for their persons and their honour.

Women shall be treated with all the regard due to their sex and shall in all cases benefit by treatment as favourable as that granted to men.

Prisoners of war shall retain the full civil capacity which they enjoyed at the time of their capture. The Detaining Power may not restrict the exercise, either within or without its own territory, of the rights such capacity confers except in so far as the captivity requires.

ARTICLE 15

The Power detaining prisoners of war shall be bound to provide free of charge for their maintenance and for the medical attention required by their state of health.

ARTICLE 17

Every prisoner of war, when questioned on the subject, is bound to give only his surname, first names and rank, date of birth, and army, regimental, personal or serial number, or failing this, equivalent information.

If he wilfully infringes this rule, he may render himself liable to a restriction of the privileges accorded to his rank or status.

Each Party to a conflict is required to furnish the persons under its jurisdiction who are liable to become prisoners of war, with an identity card showing the owner's surname, first names, rank, army, regimental, personal or serial number or equivalent information, and date of birth. The identity card may, furthermore, bear the signature or the fingerprints, or both, of the owner, and may bear, as well, any other information the Party to the conflict may wish to add concerning persons belonging to its armed forces. As far as possible the card shall measure 6.5 x 10cm and shall be issued in duplicate. The identity card shall be shown by the prisoner of war upon demand, but may in no case be taken away from him.

No physical or mental torture, nor any other form of coercion, may be inflicted on prisoners of war to secure from them information of any kind whatever. Prisoners of war who refuse to answer may not be threatened, insulted, or exposed to any unpleasant or disadvantageous treatment of any kind.

Prisoners of war who, owing to their physical or mental condition, are unable to state their identity, shall be handed over to the medical service. The identity of such prisoners shall be established by all possible means, subject to the provisions of the preceding paragraph. The questioning of prisoners of war shall be carried out in a language which they understand.

Waterboarding

Waterboarding, which simulates drowning, is a controversial technique used to extract information. It has been found that more sophisticated and positive interrogation techniques actually achieve better results.

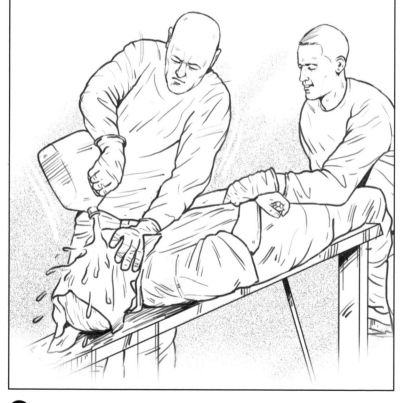

knowledge and appreciation of a culture can cause intelligence officers to change sides and become double agents.

During World War II, the British and American governments sent agents out to work with resistance groups to maintain resistance to the enemy and organize supplies. Sir Fitzroy Maclean, who had fought with the SAS in North Africa, went on a dangerous diplomatic mission to aid partisans led by Marshall Tito against the German invasion of Yugoslavia.

Interrogation

The most basic means of gathering human intelligence is to extract information from someone under some form of constraint or coercion. People of particular value in this regard may be captured Special Forces personnel or pilots or any other military personnel. Similarly, those who have been identified as terrorists themselves, or who have been associated with terrorist organizations, are also of high value for interrogation purposes. It is for this reason that a standard element in Special Forces and pilot training is resistance to interrogation (RTI).

Although torture is often cited as having been used during the interrogation of prisoners, including waterboarding (allegedly practised by some US interrogators) and the more extreme types of torture practised throughout history, including the rack and, more recently, the use of electric shocks in sensitive areas of the body, a more sophisticated and arguably more effective form of interrogation is to gain the trust of captives or to get them to reveal information without them really knowing it.

One of the main purposes of RTI training is to make military personnel aware of the pitfalls of thinking, for example, that they can handle a conversation with an interrogator and remain in control of the situation. They will also be aware of subtle forms of coercion, not amounting to torture, that can break down their will to resist or their ability to make judgments about what they should or should not say.

If a group of people have been captured, interrogators may often use supported information provided by another member of the group to entice the prisoner into thinking that the interrogator now has all the required information anyway and that there is no longer any point trying to hide it. A skilled interrogator will be aware of any subtleties in relationships between members of a group, including tensions between personalities and people of different ranks.

If a prisoner is tired after being handcuffed and blindfolded in a freezing room, the interrogator's office may offer relief from the cold and a hot drink and/or cigarette.

Sensory Deprivation

Interrogation may involve depriving captives of any sense of space or time, leaving them in a state of confusion. This prisoner is kept hooded and with his hearing obscured by ear defenders.

The difference between being in a warm room with some creature comforts, as opposed to being tied up somewhere unpleasant, may be just enough to provide the interrogator with the required lead into conversation that he has been looking for.

Major Sherwood F. Moran served with US forces during the campaign against Japan in World War II. His report on interrogation techniques, in which he pointed out that all successful interrogators were 'nice', became a classic in the field of intelligence, one that has been revisited recently after the controversial nature of so-called 'torture' techniques used by US interrogators in the War Against Terror. The following is an extract from Major Moran's report.

Suggestions for Japanese Interpreters Based on Work in the Field by Sherwood F. Moran, Major, USMC (17 July 1943)

What I have to say concretely is divided into two sections: (1) The attitude of the interpreter towards his prisoner; (2) His knowledge and use of the language.

Let us take the first one, his ATTITUDE. This is of prime importance, in many ways more important than his knowledge of the language. ...

I can simply tell you what my attitude is; I often tell a prisoner right at the start what my attitude is! I consider a prisoner (i.e. a man who has been captured and disarmed and in a perfectly safe place) as out of the war, out of the picture, and thus, in a way, not an enemy. (This is doubly so, psychologically and physically speaking, if he is wounded or starving.)
Notice that in the first part of this paragraph I used the word 'safe'. That is the point; get the prisoner to a safe place, where even he knows there is no hope of escape, that it is all over. Then forget, as it were, the 'enemy' stuff, and the 'prisoner' stuff. I tell them to forget it, telling them I am talking as a human being to a human being (ningen to shite). And they respond to this.

When it comes to the wounded, the sick, the tired, the sleepy, the starving, I consider that since they are out of the combat for good, they are simply needy human beings, needing our help, physical and spiritual. This is the standpoint of one human being thinking of another human being. But in addition, it is hard business common sense, and yields rich dividends from the Intelligence standpoint.

235

Torture

Torture can take many forms and encompasses any kind of physical or sensory pain designed to break down the captive's will to resist.

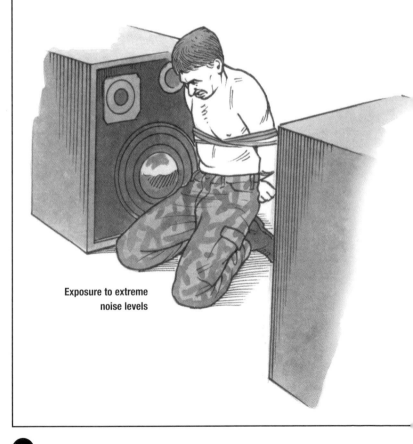

Exposure to extreme
noise levels

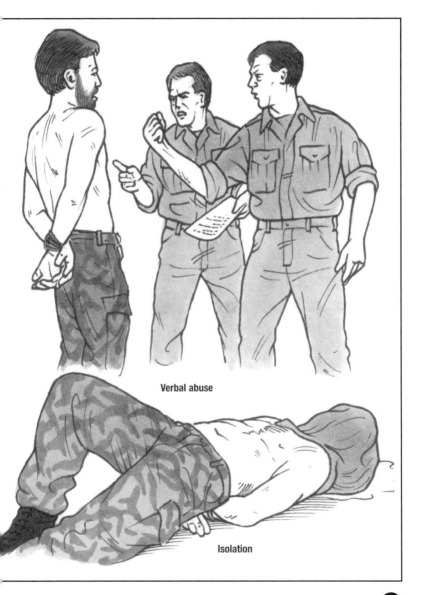

Verbal abuse

Isolation

I consider that the Japanese soldier is a person to be pitied rather than hated. I consider (and I often tell them so) that they have been led around by the nose by their leaders; that they do not know, and have not been allowed to know for over 10 years what has really been going on in the world, etc. etc. ...

But in relation to all the above, this is where 'character' comes in, that I mentioned on the preceding page. One must be absolutely sincere. I mean that one must not just assume the above attitudes in order to gain the prisoner's confidence and get him to talk. He will know the difference. You must get him to know by the expression on your face, the glance of your eye, the tone of your voice, that you do think that 'the men of the four seas are brothers,' to quote a Japanese (and Chinese) proverb (Shikai keitei). One Japanese prisoner remarked to me that he thought I was a fine gentleman ('rippana shinshi'). I think that what he was meaning to convey was that he instinctively sensed that I was sincere, was trying to be fair, and did not have it in for the Japanese as such.

One approach that is taught to Special Forces and others for resistance to interrogation is the 'grey man'. Apart from giving away his name, rank and number, according to the rules of the Geneva Convention, the prisoner remains elusive and withdrawn and apparently of little interest to the interrogator. He does not allow himself to be charmed or drawn into conversation but remains hard work until the interrogator himself tires and looks for easier prey.

The friendly/co-operative technique was used successfully by interrogators in the hunt for Saddam Hussein. This is discussed in detail in Case Study 4 in this book. In contrast, gathering the essential information that led to the identification of Osama bin Laden's hiding place is said to have resulted from coercive techniques, including waterboarding. The danger of such tactics, however, is that the prisoner may become ever more alienated and determined to resist, or he may become unconscious and even too seriously ill to be of any further use to the interrogators.

Human intelligence, in whatever form, proved vital to many of the manhunts mentioned in this book. As suspects were interviewed, they occasionally gave a hint as to the name of someone else involved, or a nickname. As each of these leads was followed up, chasing forces found themselves getting ever closer to the lair until, as with Osama bin Laden's courier, they were led directly to the leader's hideout.

Personal Qualities of an Interrogator, from US Field Manual FM 34–52

An interrogator should possess an interest in human nature and have a personality which will enable him to gain the cooperation of a source. Ideally, these and other personal qualities would be inherent in an interrogator; however, in most cases an interrogator can cultivate those qualities if he has the desire and is willing to devote time to study and practice. Some desirable personal qualities in an interrogator are discussed below.

Motivation

Motivation is the most significant factor to achieve success. Without motivation, other qualities lose their significance. The stronger the motivation, the more successful the interrogator. An interrogator may be motivated by several factors; for example:
- An interest in human relations
- A desire to react to the challenge of personal interplay
- An enthusiasm for the collection of information
- A profound interest in foreign languages and cultures

Alertness

The interrogator must be constantly aware of the shifting attitudes which normally characterize a source's reaction to interrogation. The interrogator –
Notes the source's every gesture, word, and voice inflection. Determines why the source is in a certain mood or why his mood suddenly changed. It is from the source's mood and actions the interrogator determines how to best proceed with the interrogation. Watches for any indication the source is withholding information. Watches for a tendency to resist further questioning, diminishing resistance, contradictions or other tendencies, to include susceptibility.

Personal Qualities of an Interrogator, from
US Field Manual FM 34-52 continued

Patience and Tact

The interrogator must have patience and tact in creating and maintaining rapport between himself and the source, thereby enhancing the success of the interrogation. The validity of the source's statements and motives behind these statements may be obtainable only through exercise of tact and patience. Displaying impatience may –

Encourage the difficult source to think if he remains unresponsive for a little longer, the interrogator will stop questioning.

Cause the source to lose respect for the interrogator, thereby reducing his effectiveness.

An interrogator, with patience and tact, is able to terminate an interrogation and later continue it without arousing apprehension or resentment.

Credibility

The interrogator must maintain credibility with the source and friendly forces. Failure to produce material rewards when promised may adversely affect future interrogations. The importance of accurate reporting cannot be overstressed, since interrogation reports are often the basis for tactical decisions and operations.

Objectivity

The interrogator must maintain an objective and dispassionate attitude, regardless of the emotional reactions he may actually experience or simulate during the interrogation. Without objectivity, he may unconsciously distort the information acquired. He may also be unable to vary his interrogation technique effectively.

Self-Control

The interrogator must have exceptional self-control to avoid displays of genuine anger, irritation, sympathy, or weariness which may cause him to lose the initiative during the interrogation. Self-control is especially important when employing interrogation techniques which require the display of simulated emotions or attitudes.

Adaptability

An interrogator must adapt to the many and varied personalities which he will encounter. He should try to imagine himself in the source's position. By being adaptable, he can smoothly shift his techniques and approaches during interrogations according to the operational environment. In many cases, he has to conduct interrogations under unfavourable physical conditions.

CASE STUDY 5:

The Hunt for Abu Musab al-Zarqawi

Abu Musab al-Zarqawi was considered to be one of the most dangerous al-Qaeda militants in Iraq. Born in Jordan in 1966, and having left school early in order to become a street thug, al-Zarqawi is believed to have become fully embedded in al-Qaeda after a visit to Afghanistan in 1989 where he ran a paramilitary training camp. He was imprisoned in Jordan for about nine years, after which he committed some of his most notable and public attacks against US and allied forces, the United Nations and civilians. His extreme violence included suicide bombings and publicized executions of hostages, some of which he performed personally. The US Government put a $25 million bounty on his head. Either personally or through his spider-web of contacts, al-Zarqawi was simply the most dangerous terrorist alive after Osama bin Laden himself.

Task Force 145

From the Allies' point of view, which in Iraq effectively meant US and British forces, the search for al-Zarqawi was a number one priority manhunt which would be allocated the highest level intelligence resources and special

Joint Special Forces Operations Command was established to maximize interoperability between the different US special operations forces.

operations personnel in a group known as Task Force 145.

The work of Task Force 145 was often painstakingly deliberate but it could also provide a hair-trigger response when required and act with extreme decisiveness. It called on a range of assets, including US military intelligence, incorporating also Intelligence Support Activity (ISA) and the CIA Special Activities Division, British intelligence, Army 1st Special Forces Operational Detachment-Delta, US Navy SEAL Team 6 (Special Warfare Development Group), 75th Ranger Regiment, 160th Special Operations Aviation Regiment, British 22 Special Air Service, Special Boat Squadron, Special Reconnaissance Regiment and Special Forces Support Group. The umbrella for Task Force 145 was US Joint Special Operations Command (JSOC). The unit was divided into Task Force Center, Task Force West and Task Force North. Task Force Black was the British and US element.

Although al-Zarqawi as an individual took a long time to run to ground, Task Force Black on its own is credited with capturing or eliminating at least 3500 terrorists from the streets of Baghdad. Part of the reason for the success was the unrelenting momentum maintained by the Special Forces and their intelligence back-up teams, which became known as 'the unblinking eye'.

Interrogation Techniques

Meanwhile, behind the scenes, interrogators (or 'gators' as they were sometimes known in US military parlance) were methodically working their way through suspects, pooling information, making connections, not letting small details pass them by and occasionally making a significant breakthrough.

Task Force 145 could see that traditional rough interrogation tactics were not only getting them nowhere, but in fact they might have been pushing them into reverse. Cue the arrival of Matthew Alexander, an interrogator in the mould of some of the most sophisticated, and highly successful, interrogators throughout history.

Matthew Alexander flew out with a team of interrogators to Baghdad in March 2006. At a briefing on arrival, they were told that al-Zarqawi had made it his mission to create a civil war between the Sunni and the Shia, and that al-Zarqawi was an even bigger priority than Osama bin Laden. Alexander and his team began with a series of clever ploys against the al-Qaeda prisoners, including using their love for their families as a means of leveraging information. Another method was rapid-fire questioning. A series of short, sharp questions were asked at high speed so that the detainee begins to lose his ability to think straight. The questions continued at such a pace that the detainee began to 'trip over his lies' and discrepancies begin to appear, which are then picked up and thrown back at him. Soon, the interrogators had discovered the locations of safe houses where suicide bombers were waiting to carry out their terrorist attacks.

Nothing is more important in Arab culture than family. Their family bonds are even stronger than in the West and no Iraqi would be willing to betray his family. Alexander used this ruse against a detainee called Abu Gamal, by telling him he wanted to help him get back to his family. He worked on Gamal's natural concern for his family by asking who was protecting them.

The next ruse was that Gamal was told that he was effectively in competition with other detainees who are simultaneously being questioned elsewhere. That meant he needed to get a move on to reveal the necessary information and stop lying – otherwise he would be the loser. Ruses such as use of such deceptions were mixed with hard facts, such as when Gamal was told that the penalty for assisting suicide bombers was death by hanging.

The next day it was back to the emotional ploys. This time, Alexander went directly for the jugular and conjured up an image of Gamal's wife's face, which was smiling until she learnt that Gamal was involved with suicide bombers who planned to kill women and children. Unfortunately, this failed to work as expected, for Gamal had two wives and did not know which one to imagine. However, the fact that he had two wives gave Alexander leverage in another way. Both of Gamal's wives turned out to be expensive to keep, having a predilection for clothes and jewellery. It became clear that Gamal had joined al-Qaeda because he needed the money, so therefore the leverage would be offering to help him with his financial needs.

At the next interview, Alexander had $10,000 on his desk, which had been taken in a raid. He also

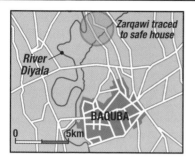

River Diyala

Zarqawi traced to safe house

BAQUBA

0   5km

It was patient and skilful interrogation work that pinpointed the safe house occupied by al-Zarqawi.

forged a divorce petition that indicated to Gamal that he could get rid of the more expensive of his wives. Suddenly, Gamal started talking in detail about his work as a bomb-maker for al-Qaeda. As the interrogations continued, the interrogators found themselves getting ever closer to the prime object of the manhunt – al Zarqawi.

Elimination of Al-Zarqawi

The key to the investigation and the lead to al-Zarqawi appeared to be the Group of Five, which was headed up by one of the detainees, Abu Raja. Somehow, a ladder needed to be constructed that would lead from the Group of Five to al-Zarqawi himself.

Another important aspect of Arab culture, apart from the family, is respect for authority. There is a natural instinct to revere authority figures and to treat them with respect. In one interview, one of the interrogators said she would speak to her 'boss' to engineer a special deal with him. The role of the 'boss' was played by Alexander, who came in with a clipboard and pen, looking sceptical, busy and exuding authority. The detainee was convinced and treated Alexander with deference. Alexander said he could help him if he would just let him know who he worked for. The detainee fell for it. The man he named was Abu Raja, who was already in custody.

Whenever there was any form of lead, the team of Special Forces from Task Force 145 travelled out to locations by helicopter, sitting on side-mounted benches above the skids. They stormed buildings with only a split second to decide whether or not to pull their triggers when they entered. Sometimes they found nothing more than innocent civilians. At other times, however, they came across suicide bombers. Sometimes, they found a useful piece of evidence such as a DVD.

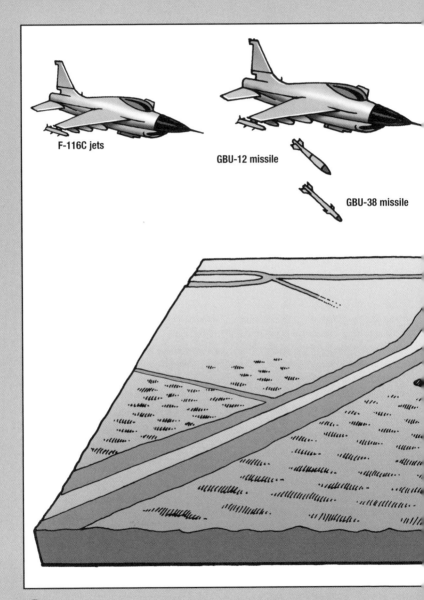

F-116C jets

GBU-12 missile

GBU-38 missile

Hitting the Target

Once al-Zarqawi's location had been verified by Special Forces, two USAF F-16 fighter bombers attacked the house with guided weapons.

rget

Timeline

30 October 1966: Abu Musab al-Zarqawi born in Zarqa, Jordan.

1999: Al-Zarqawi attempts to blow up Radisson SAS hotel in Amman.

2002: US diplomat murdered in Jordan in plot organized by Al-Zarqawi.

2003: Al-Zarqawi organizes bomb attacks in Casablanca, Morocco.

19 August 2003: Al-Zarqawi responsible for Canal Hotel Bombing on United Nations HQ in Iraq, killing UN Secretary-General's special envoy Sergio Vieira de Mello and 21 others.

2004: Al-Zarqawi joins al-Qaeda.

September 2005: Al-Zarqawi declares war on the Shia in Iraq.

7 June 2006: Al-Zarqawi killed by bombs dropped by USAF F16C fighter. Also killed is his spiritual adviser Sheik Abd-al-Rahman.

Al-Zarqawi's hideout was relatively close to Baghdad, which allowed him to direct terrorist operations from close quarters.

A twist in the story by one of the senior detainees suggested that another detainee, Abu Bayda, who was well spoken with a British accent and also highly intelligent, was something more than what he claimed to be – just a cameraman. Alexander interviewed Abu Bayda, using all of his skills to earn his respect by focusing especially on his respect for his religion and culture, and finally elicited a vital name – Abu Ayyub al Masri. They had just moved one more rung up the ladder and were now only one step behind al-Zarqawi himself. Alexander continued to probe Abu Bayda, this time with an awareness of the Iraqi culture of conspiracy. An intelligent Iraqi like Abu Bayda would be naturally drawn to a plausible and successful conspiracy. Ultimately, Abu Bayda delivered an essential clue – that Sheikh Abu Abd al-Rahman was the key to getting to al-Zarqawi for he was his spiritual adviser. Abu Bayda said that if Abd al-Rahman stopped to change cars he was on the way to see al-Zarqawi.

From that moment onwards, Task Force 145 concentrated their surveillance assets onto al Rahman and watched his movements like a hawk. Special Forces soldiers were on hair-trigger response as the movements of the cars were monitored. At last, the blue car made its way to an isolated house and the passenger in the car stepped out. Suddenly, two USAF F-16C jets appeared overhead and the lead jet then dropped two 230kg (500lb) guided bombs, a laser-guided GBU-12 and GPS-guided GBU-38 on the building. Al-Zarqawi and some members of his family were killed in the attack. Another manhunt was over.

In a military manhunt on the ground, ultimately there will come a point when the tracking team and their associated support close in on the enemy. In this chapter we will look at the various ways in which trackers intercept an enemy, whether in a countryside or urban environment, and whether they are using traditional tracking skills or high-tech assets.

Tracking a Target with Anticipation

The obvious advantage a tracker has is that his quarry is a human being like himself. If the quarry is in a rush to escape, he may do obvious things or take the shortest route. Equally, if he does not know he is being followed, he may take the obvious route and all the tracker needs to ask himself is which way he would have gone in the circumstances. Sometimes this will be entirely apparent due to obstacles in the path and so on.

If the quarry does know he is being followed and the tracker knows that too, it may require some more sophisticated thinking to work out what less obvious things the quarry

• •

When making the final approach to the target, extreme caution must be used to remain out of sight and not to make noise. Dogs may be used to attack and hold the target.

5

A successful manhunt will inevitably lead to final approach and contact with the target.

Route Planning

When planning an approach to a target, the route needs to be carefully planned so as to maximize available cover. Soldiers may make a sketch of the area to ensure all bases are covered.

might have done or less obvious routes he may have taken. A good tracker will be instinctively aware of areas where the quarry may have tried to throw him off the scent and will examine all of the options carefully. Typical attempts to throw the tracker off course include backtracking, as has been described in the chapter 'Training'.

If there is a loss of track, Special Forces are trained to run through a set procedure to minimize the time lost. Assuming there is a group of soldiers on the trail, they move back and go into a defensive position in case the incident site has been deliberately set up for an ambush.

They then conduct a search in a looping fashion to try to find any entry and exit points from the incident area. At this point, the tracker will often make a sketch of the area, to mark the entry and exit points and any other signs.

Use of Dogs

Dogs have been used for tracking for many centuries and more recently have been used by the Germans in World War II to track down Allied airmen who had crashed or parachuted into enemy territory, and other Allied personnel. The Germans used German Shepherds, which were taught both to track and attack the quarry.

The British learned from the German experience and trained dogs for tracking and other purposes through the Royal Army Veterinary Corps. The British tended to favour dogs such as Labradors for tracking, and put greater emphasis on the tracking than the attack.

It is a common belief that you can confuse a dog and put it off its scent by doing several things. The most popular notion is that by using a strong-smelling substance, like pepper for example, the dog will quickly lose the scent. However, the reality is that the dog is likely to sneeze out the pepper particles and have an even sharper nose than before.

The next well-known stratagem is to try running across a stream or river, as the water will not hold the scent. This is true to the extent that the water itself will not hold it, but it is most likely that the evader will need to climb out the other side at some point and the dog will simply run up and down the bank until it finds that point. There may also be visible clues of somebody having clambered out to confirm the point for the dog handler.

Occasionally the dog may be given scents related to the evader that reinforce its scent and sense of direction. This may be anything the evader has either handled or worn. Apart from the scent of the actual evader, which is left on the ground or in the air, the dog can also follow the scent of disturbed vegetation as a back-up. This is the scent equivalent

Tracker Dogs

Dogs can be used for trailing a target with both ground and air scent as well as for attack. They are a formidable asset for tracking. These are the breeds most commonly used as tracker dogs.

Labrador

Doberman

Alsatian

Standing Orders – Roger's Rangers (1736)

- Don't forget nothing.
- Have your musket clean as a whistle, hatchet scoured, 60 rounds powder and ball, and be ready to march at a minute's warning.
- When you're on the march, act the way you would if you was sneaking up on a deer. See the enemy first.
- Tell the truth about what you see and do. There is an army depending on us for correct information. You can lie all you please when you tell other folks about the Rangers, but don't never lie to a Ranger or officer.
- Don't never take a chance you don't have to.
- When we're on the march we march single file, far enough apart so one shot can't go through two men.
- If we strike swamps, or soft ground, we spread out abreast, so it's hard to track us.
- When we march, we keep moving till dark, so as to give the enemy the least possible chance at us.
- When we camp, half the party stays awake while the other half sleeps.
- If we take prisoners, we keep 'em separate til we have had time to examine them, so they can't cook up a story between 'em.

of seeing a path through vegetation. Even the human nose can smell freshly mown grass so imagine how easy it is for the dog to pick up the smell of various bits of crushed vegetation with its infinitely more powerful nose.

Dogs do have their limitations and they cannot be expected in all environments to work miracles. Once a dog is tired, it may fail to follow a scent efficiently, so it either needs to be rested before moving on or another dog brought in. Dogs can be rendered almost useless in a battle scenario with intense noise going on, and they also find it difficult to distinguish between friend and foe. So a patrol that is moving with a dog needs not to position itself in such a way that the dog thinks the patrol is the quarry. The dog cannot track

- Don't ever march home the same way. Take a different route so you won't be ambushed.
- No matter whether we travel in big parties or little ones, each party has to keep a scout 20 yards ahead, 20 yards on each flank and 20 yards in the rear, so the main body can't be surprised and wiped out.
- Every night you'll be told where to meet if surrounded by a superior force.
- Don't sit down to eat without posting sentries.
- Don't sleep beyond dawn. Dawn's when the French and Indians attack.
- Don't cross a river by a regular ford.
- If somebody's trailing you, make a circle, come back onto your own tracks, and ambush the folks that aim to ambush you.
- Don't stand up when the enemy's coming against you. Kneel down. Hide behind a tree.
- Let the enemy come till he's almost close enough to touch. Then let him have it and jump out and finish him up with your hatchet.

equally well in any conditions and the evader may be able to take advantage of this when trying to get away.

Ideal conditions for a dog include:

- Approximately equal air and ground temperatures.
- Mild temperatures without too much sun and a fairly slow evaporation.
- Shade provided by trees and other vegetation.

- Obvious signs left by the quarry such as blood, hair or pieces of torn clothing.
- A running evader who is giving off a lot of body odour due to exertion.
- An evader who is generally dirty and smelly.
- An evader moving at speed who causes a great deal of disturbance in the vegetation.

Evading Dogs

Crossing streams or rivers is often regarded as a good way of evading dogs. However, a dog is often able to pick up the scent at the exit point from the water.

Picking up Scents

Once a dog has been given the scent of something belonging to the target, it will be able to follow that particular scent both in the air and on the ground through either urban or rural environments. This makes the dog a formidable opponent.

Dog Facts

There are different theories about how long a dog remains efficient in pursuit, taking into account the fact that the dog is using a high-level sensory capacity alongside physical movement in pursuit of a quarry.

- Dog speed:
  The maximum speed dogs can run is about 64km/h (40mph) but this can only be sustained for relatively short distances – 100m (328ft) or so. Their average pace over longer distances may be about 16km/h (10mph) but, of course, they are limited by the speed of their two-legged hand.
- Dog sight:
  The dog's vision is not particularly remarkable or different to that of a human. Dogs are particularly good at spotting movement but otherwise they appear only to be able to see in black and white and have average night vision.
- Dog hearing:
  Dogs have very good hearing, which is about 40 times superior to that of the human ear. With their large ears, which they cock to capture nuances of sound, dogs can also accurately pinpoint the direction of sound, which makes it even more difficult for a quarry to remain undetected. Dogs have the ability to shut out their inner ear and filter out distracting sounds.
- Dog smell:
  Dogs have a superb sense of smell. Their sense of smell is at least 900 times more efficient than that of a human. In view of this, it is almost impossible for an evader to imagine how he should evade a dog because, of course, humans tend only to smell obvious things such as body odour, when a person is present, or deodorants or a wide range of obvious chemicals. It would not occur to the average human that a dog can actually smell microscopic particles that fall from the body, such as skin or hair particles, and that these can either be picked up on the ground or in the air.

Dogs Tracking

A well-trained dog and handler team can lead soldiers quickly to a target, although there are methods of slowing them down.

The dog can, however, be challenged and maybe even defeated by the following conditions:

- Hot sun.
- Strong wind.
- Heavy rain.
- A road where cars regularly pass.
- Running water (though remember that a dog is able to pick up the scent again where the evader has climbed out of a river or stream).
- Fire.
- Confusion with animal scent. For example, an evader may try to mingle with livestock so that his scent is lost, but a good tracker dog should be able to pick the scent up again if it circles the area.

The dog needs to be on the case as soon as possible in order to take maximum advantage of the scent trail and to increase the possibility of catching up with the quarry. Anything that is associated with the evader should be left alone so that the dog does not get confused with different scents.

Evading dogs

Although it is difficult to throw a well-trained dog off the scent completely, evaders can use certain tactics that help to delay both the dog and the handler, such as:

- Creating an erratic path by doubling back and going round vegetation. This can cause

Evading Dogs

**Tracker dogs
work best when
following a single,
unbroken line of
scent. By winding
your route around
obstacles and by
crossing water, you
can either make
the dog turn back
on itself, or lose
your track entirely.**

confusion and may even tangle the lead between the handler and the dog.

- Move in the same direction as the wind, so the body scent is blown away from the pursuers.
- Cross obstacles that will delay both dog and handler. Climbing over a fence is one example.

- Change direction unexpectedly and in places where this would not be obvious.
- Use water obstacles where appropriate – but always bear in mind that it will be more difficult afterwards to run in wet clothing. It is important to try to exit from the water onto

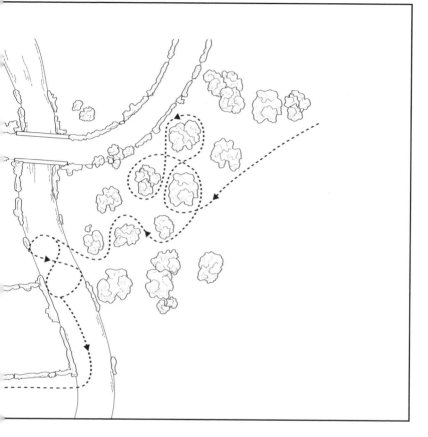

a hard surface to minimize the sign that is left.

- If it is possible to find one, use a bicycle on a hard surface or take a ride on an animal such as a horse or donkey.
- Mix with other people or try to pass through areas where other people have passed.

Final Approach

Once the position of the quarry has been identified, it may be necessary to make a final, stealthy approach, assuming the quarry is not aware of the presence of the tracking team.

In the countryside, stealthy final approaches make use of ground as well as camouflage. Movement has to be carefully controlled and painstaking. As snipers know, even a small distance on the ground may take a considerable amount of time to cross. Moving in a stealthy way requires a considerable amount of physical fitness, because the muscles are used to hold the body steady in slow movements in unfamiliar and often uncomfortable postures.

Assuming the quarry is keeping a lookout and may be wary, it is usually not a good idea to approach directly in front, and preferable to go round, perhaps approaching from the flank. The chaser will always be looking ahead, aiming for the best bits of cover while also taking extreme care not to cause either noise or movement in the vegetation around him. For example, to move a long piece of grass or a branch will send a signal to a walking quarry that someone or something is present and put him on his guard.

Each time the chaser moves, he needs to be aware of where the quarry might be situated and what his arcs of vision are. The chaser must also always be aware of the possibility of the quarry being closer than he thought.

If walking as well as crawling, the chaser needs to be aware of dry twigs or leaves or anything else that might alert the quarry to his presence. Mud can also be a danger, as it sometimes makes a sucking noise when the foot is lifted.

Bin Laden latest:

All information gathered points to the fact that a very important person lives in this house – but who is it?

Stalking crouch

As the chaser gets closer to where he knows the quarry is or where he thinks he might be, the chaser can move from an upright position to a more crouched position – the upright or stalking crouch. Lean your body forward, keeping your head low, and rest your hands above your knees. Keep the knees slightly bent and make sure the feet are lifted well off the ground for each step.

When placing your foot on the ground, start with the outside edge of the foot and then roll carefully into the ball of your foot before bringing down the heel, taking care at all times to be aware of any twigs or leaves that may make a noise.

It is quite difficult to walk in a crouched position and it is a good idea to practise as much as possible before doing it for real.

A Selection from SAS Rules for Lead Scouts and Jungle Soldiers in the Jungle

LEAD SCOUTS AND JUNGLE SOLDIERS

• Do not 'sign post' your routes.

• Always move with stealth and never at such a speed that your presence in the area is telegraphed ahead of your visible distance.

• When faced with thick undergrowth, if possible go around. If you have to go through, weave your way under or over. Never cut or allow your pack or body to get caught up in the branches or vines and so cause sounds and movement at the tops of young trees.

• Remember that the sound made by the rattle from poorly packed equipment, unnecessary talking above a whisper, a cough or a broken stick will travel outwards in all directions.

• Never forget your own 'sign'-leaving tendency; ground sign, top sign, and the phantom twig snapper. If necessary detail Tail End Charlie to brush over and camouflage your tracks. Always consider the possibility of using deception tactics.

• Always vary your route and timings, out and back from all patrols; unless you want to be ambushed.

• Always remember that as the Lead Scout, it is your responsibility to ensure that you do not lead your patrol into the killing zone of an enemy ambush. Make use of the 'listening halts'. Develop all your senses to a high pitch and if ever you become suspicious of the area ahead, stop the patrol and have a 'listening halt' or go forward and check it out with your cover man. Look through not at the vegetation and undergrowth to the second or third layer.

A Selection from SAS Rules for Lead Scouts and Jungle Soldiers in the Jungle (continued)

- Observe and become familiar with the natural, sights and smells of the insect world, the animal kingdom, the bird life and all forms of vegetation in your area of operations. Be alert to any sign, which indicates man's presence in the area.

- On all suspicious sights, sounds and smells, react as the wild animal does and remain perfectly still. If an enemy appears and moves across your front, there is a very good chance that he will not see you. If the enemy appears to be walking towards you, slowly and silently go down on one knee, at the same time bring your weapon into the shoulder aimed at the approaching sound, or carry out Immediate Action drills.

- Always make positive identification before shooting.

- When camping, selection of the site will be in such a place that a surprise night attack would be impossible. Use hammocks for camps on near-vertical slopes or crawl into the centre of thick, noise-making

Feline crawl

As you get closer to the quarry, you need to keep your head lower to ensure you are not seen, although this may depend on the kind of cover between yourself and the quarry.

In this position, the head is the highest point on the body and the rest of the body is kept as low as possible. When moving either hands or knees, use the same principle as when walking in a crouch – move very carefully and feel for anything that might cause a noise, such as twigs or leaves.

When stalking its prey, a cat places the back foot in the same place that the front foot has occupied. The advantages of this style of movement are that the ground has been tested and firmed down by the front foot vegetation. No lights, no noise, no cooking and all unused equipment to be replaced in bergens.

• Again when operating as an information gathering patrol, avoid all contact with the enemy. The deeper you get into his secure areas the more relaxed he becomes and so the easier for you to observe and gain intelligence of his movements and activities. Do not leave tracks or signs to tell him that you are in his area. Do not use tracks or trails – loop them.

The maxim for the modern soldier is:
Once on patrol
Switch on
Stay switched on.
Remember
There is always someone ready
To switch you off
PERMANENTLY!

and it reduces by half the potential for stepping on something noisy. It is not nearly so easy for a human to achieve this, as you have to place a knee in the position that had been occupied by the hand and you need to avoid dragging the foot, but, as with all of these methods, practice will make it easier and, ultimately, the fitter you are, the smoother your movements will be.

Flat crawl

Once you get very close to the quarry and so are now in danger of being seen, the flat crawl allows you to move while completely flat on the ground. Move into the flat-crawl position by allowing the forward part of your body to move forward and down, taking care not to create any noise as your belly touches the ground.

Stalking

When close to the target, it is important to keep the head and body as low as possible. This starts with a stalking crouch, through a feline crawl to the flat crawl.

Feline crawl

Flat crawl

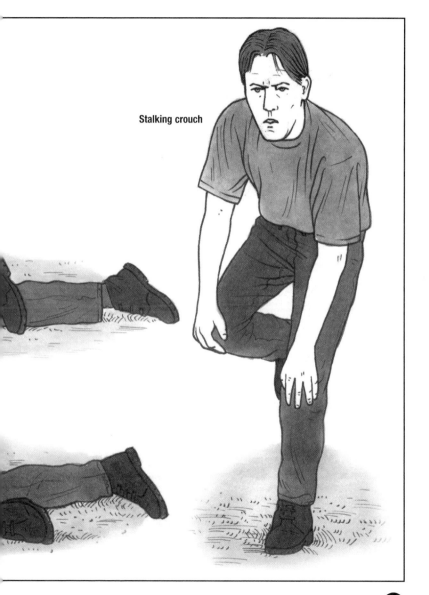

Stalking crouch

The flat crawl is the most difficult movement because it places a strain on muscles that are not normally used in this way. First, place your weight on your forearms and then on your feet and lower legs to provide enough lift to move forward slightly. You need to judge how far you can realistically move in this way and over what span of time, as it will take a long time to cover a small amount of ground.

Freezing

Many children's games incorporate natural stealth tactics. Grandmother's footsteps is a game where you have to freeze stock-still if the person you are following turns round. This ability to freeze is useful when approaching a quarry, as movement can attract attention and it may be that the quarry looks in your direction while you are in the process of moving.

Again, it is worth practising this, as it requires a high degree of muscle control and balance to suddenly stop the body in mid-movement and hold the position for as long as necessary. It helps, therefore, to make sure that when you move you are moving, always stay in balance so that when you suddenly have to stop you do not teeter.

Sometimes, after freezing, you may then find that you need to move back into a position where you are concealed, and you have to judge when you can do this with very slow and fluid movements.

Using sound as cover

One of the many instinctive tricks you may discover as you become more experienced is how to use other sounds as a cover for movement. There may be a gust of wind that rustles leaves in the trees, allowing you to move forward with more sound cover. Alternatively, it may be an animal or bird sound or a car passing or plane flying overhead.

Avoiding noise

The other side of the sound issue is making noise yourself. You should check your pockets for anything that may rattle and ensure your watch or any other electronic equipment does not have an alarm set or is switched off.

Also be aware of the kind of clothing you are wearing, as some fabrics tend to cause rustling noises. It is not always possible to tell if any is present, but if possible try to avoid disturbing any wildlife. Birds bursting out of a covert or trees tend to indicate the presence of something or someone. If animals are disturbed, keep very still until the quarry has had a chance to ascertain that everything is OK before moving on.

When communicating with other members of a team, it is important to use hand signals rather than your voice. Special Forces will have a known set of hand signals for such purposes and, otherwise, hand signals should be agreed and rehearsed before the mission.

Noise Reduction

When walking at night, it is important to test the ground carefully with your foot, beginning with the side and front of the foot and gently feeling for any material that may cause noise as the foot is lowered.

Hand Signals

It is vital to understand hand signals in close proximity to the target, as these enable signals to be given silently.

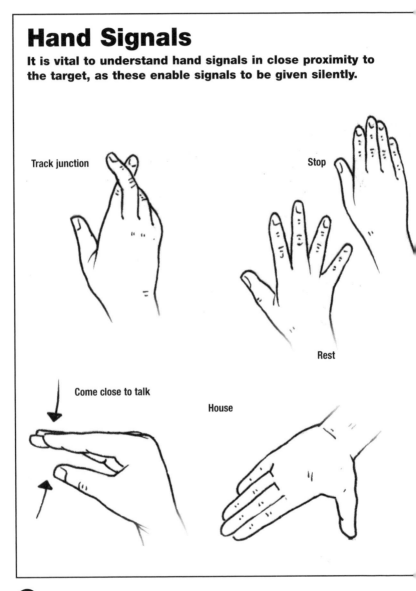

Track junction

Stop

Rest

Come close to talk

House

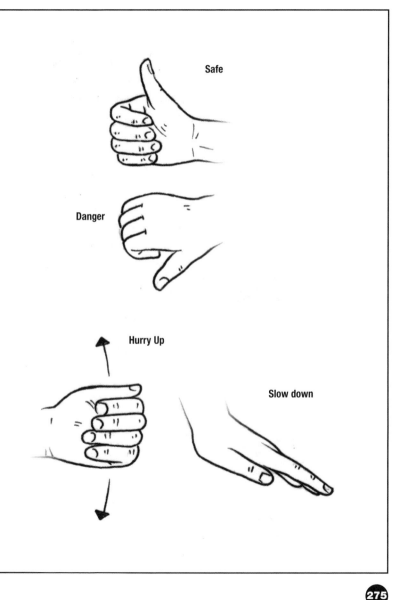

Safe

Danger

Hurry Up

Slow down

Hand Signals (continued)

**It is important to be alert
to both hand and head
signals, as they provide
vital information when
close to the target.**

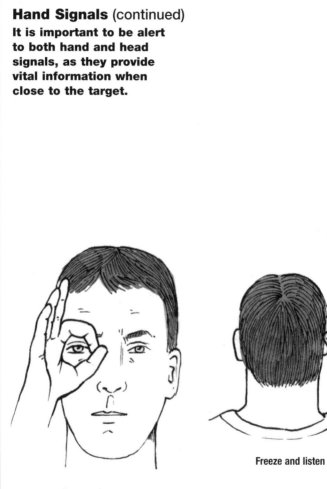

Reconnaisance

Freeze and listen

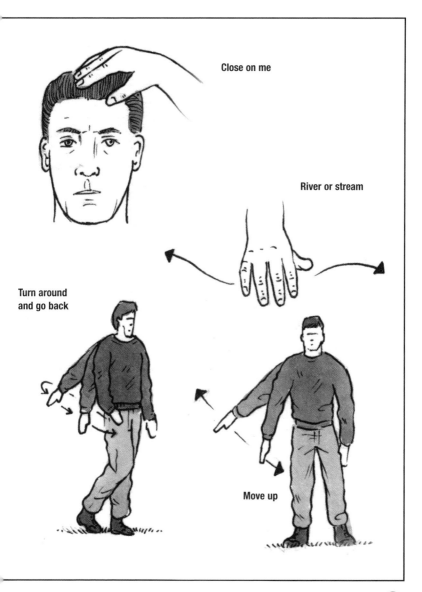

Close on me

River or stream

Turn around
and go back

Move up

Watching and Waiting

It may come to the point when the tracker has got into a position where he has identified the quarry's position but just needs to watch and wait to see if there is any movement.

Remaining still and incognito is a skill in itself, and can be practised. Because we are normally in the habit of moving about in various ways, keeping silent and still demands quite a lot of self-control. Being still and unseen can be practised almost anywhere and, after a while, natural events take place around you as animals and birds either become comfortable with your presence or do not notice it.

The following recommendations come from a Rhodesian Counter-

Covert Surveillance

Observation may require long periods before any movement is spotted. A soldier could be forced to stay in this position for days on end, so a great deal of stamina is essential.

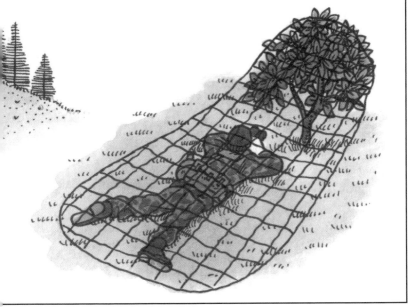

Insurgency Manual on setting ambushes against terrorists:

1. **Aim.** The aim of an ambush is to surprise and eliminate the enemy on ground and in circumstances of the military forces' own choosing.

2. **Intelligence.** The majority of ambushes are laid as a result of:

   a. Intelligence gained through direct or indirect information from surrendered or captured terrorists, agents and informers.

   b. Chance information.

   c. An appreciation of likely terrorist movement and activity based on familiarity with an area, coupled with the pattern of terrorist movement in the area concerned.

3. **Purpose.** An ambush may be

Firing Positions

**It is important to adopt a
good firing position, with
as much of the body
concealed as possible
before engaging a target.**

designed to eliminate either individuals or groups of the enemy. Enemy movement may not take place at the time anticipated, and the enemy may use civilians to watch for signs of military forces activity and ambush positions. Commanders must always remember this and not become discouraged if a carefully laid ambush fails to achieve its objects. A clear distinction must, however, be drawn between such failures and ambushes that are in the right place at the right time, but fail because of mismanagement.

4. **Composition**.

   a. Ambushes may vary in size from a small four-man affair laid as part of a patrol operation, to a major operation involving a platoon/company group. The guiding principle will be economy of force. The smaller the force, the easier it will be to introduce it into the ambush area, to control the operation and to extricate the ambush force after contact.

   b. It is essential that the best possible team is chosen for each ambush. This may frequently entail a troop/company commander commanding an ambush group, although it may only consist of a handful of men. Men especially selected for their marksmanship or other particular qualities should be drawn from any element of the unit. The overriding consideration in selecting the ambush party should be to choose the troop most likely to succeed in that particular case.

5. **The principles of ambushing.** Instantaneous co-ordinated action against a surprised enemy held within a well-covered killing ground is essential for success. This requires fulfilment of the following conditions:

   a. A high standard of training in ambush techniques.

   b. Careful planning and execution.

   c. First-class security in all stages.

   d. Concealment of all signs of the occupation of the position.

   e. An intelligent layout and siting.

   f. A high standard of battle discipline, particularly by night.

   g. Determination by all troopers of the ambush party to wait and kill.

   h. A simple clear-cut plan for springing the ambush.

   i. Good shooting from all positions: kneeling, sitting, standing, lying and from behind cover.

   j. Surprise, the key to successful ambushes.

   k. Safety of own forces

Route Planning

Due to the nature of the final approach to a quarry, you need to keep your head down, and so it is difficult to plan the route and see your way forward. As much preparation as possible will, therefore, be helpful. It is important to work out an approach that makes best

Final Approach

When making an arrest, it is important to consider whether the target is hiding a gun in his pocket or elsewhere.

Applying Face Camouflage

Face camouflage is a vital part of a soldier's preparation for operations, as it breaks up the contours of the face and reduces the glow of skin.

use of available cover and, according to the type of cover, you need to work out what kind of movement will be involved. For example, if there is a high hedgerow, a crouched position may be appropriate, allowing you to move fairly quickly. If there is only a ditch, however, you will need to be able to crouch, and this will obviously take much longer. When planning the route, take note of any awkward danger points such as gaps between hedges or where a ditch flattens out because the quarry may be watching such points carefully. You should learn to recognize where there is dead ground, as again this will allow you to move with relative freedom and speed.

Occasionally, you will need to double-check your route and watch for any signs of movement by the quarry. Choose a spot where you can peer through cover, such as a hedge, without raising your head above it.

As you get closer to the quarry, noise and smell become more important, particularly at night when noise and scent carry further and the senses are more attuned to both due to reduced vision. Make sure you have not used any strong anti-perspirant or aftershave and ensure that there is nothing loose in your pockets that will create noise.

A flash or glint of reflected sunlight or moonlight off the face of a watch or metal object may be enough to alert the quarry to your presence

and may put you in great danger if he is armed. During World War II, during the battle for Stalingrad, a top Russian sniper killed his German adversary because of a momentary glint of sunlight reflected off his binoculars. Obviously, it is not advisable to use a flashlight or stop for a cigarette break!

Depending on what kind of camouflage you are using, you may need to change it if the vegetation you are passing through changes. As mentioned above, take care also to camouflage any exposed parts of your face and hands with camouflage cream.

The Attack

If the final approach to a quarry is one-on-one, decisions will have to be made according to whether the quarry is armed or whether the chaser is armed. The chaser may have access to a back-up team or may be able to call in some other form of asset, such as aerial support.

If the quarry is known to be armed and the chaser is part of a team, they will want to position themselves in such a way as to provide adequate covering fire if the quarry should resist.

If it is a military operation, there may be aerial photography or a map of the area. If this is the case, the tracker will need to examine these to determine which are the best approaches to the quarry and to identify possible escape routes.

Field Planning

Before making the final approach to the target, all possible approach routes need to be considered through careful observation. By using a simple 180° clock system, the soldier can identify positions to his colleagues.

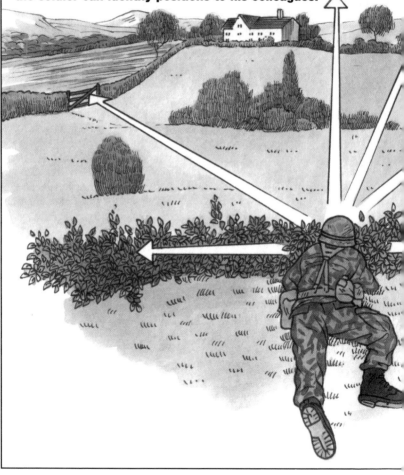

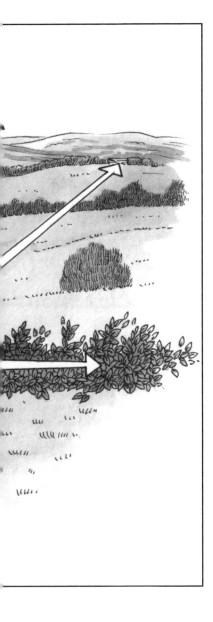

If the tracker has a support team, he or the commander will position covering forces to block any potential escape routes.

The Selous Scouts had the following recommendations for planning and preparation prior to an attack:

1. **Introduction.** *To ensure a successful operation, the planning and preparation for such an operation are most important. When speed is essential for success, it may be necessary to sacrifice security to a certain extent. The commander concerned must carefully consider this aspect when making his appreciation.*

2. **Appreciation.** *Depending on the time available, the commander responsible for the operation must make a careful, detailed appreciation based on the task. This appreciation must include such factors as the enemy, the local population, the terrain and own forces.*

3. **Enemy.** *in the appreciation, points regarding the enemy which must be taken into consideration are the following:*
   a. *Nature and strength.*
   b. *Routes both in and out normally used by the enemy.*
   c. *In and out timings normally used by the enemy for his movement to and from the objective.*
   d. *security measures such as location and routine of sentries, defensive system, patrols,*

sighting of weapons, alert and alarm systems, etc.
e. Normal reactions to security force presence.
f. Possible additional or external support that may be provided.

4. **Local population.** When considering the local population, the following aspects must be considered:
a. Density and concentration.
b. The nature and type of the village or settlement and its location in relation to the objective.
c. The attitude of the local population towards both the enemy and security forces.
d. The daily routing of the local population and routes or paths normally used by them to their cultivations and water points.

5. **Terrain.** when considering terrain, the following aspects must be borne in mind:
1. Nature and size and exact location of the objective.
2. Nature of the terrain around the objective, this to include:
i. Position in relation to the objective.
ii. Observation and fields of fire.
iii. Obstacles, either natural or man-made.
iv. Cover and concealment.
v. Approaches and exit/escape routes.
vi. Checkpoints.

Sources of information. The above information about the terrain can be obtained by the following means:
a. Patrolling.
b. Air and ground reconnaissance.
c. Maps and air photographs.
d. Local population, police, informers or captured enemy, etc.

Timings. In determining H-hour, the following aspects must be considered:
0. Time available in which to carry out the operation.
1. Distances to be covered by attacking force.
2. Using cover of darkness for approach march for maximum security.
3. Enemy sentry routine, i.e., early morning when sentries may not yet have been posted or are still sleepy from the night before, or at last light when sentries may be withdrawn.
4. Taking advantage of bad weather conditions, rest and meal times.
5. The possibility of attacking during the hours of darkness, bearing in mind the attendant advantages and disadvantages.

Routes. When considering the approach and withdrawal routes, the following should be borne in mind:
0. Distances to be covered by the various groups.
1. Secrecy and security.
2. Nature of the route, i.e., easy or difficult going.

Special Forces Ambush

An ambush has to be carefully set up to cover all possible escape routes for an enemy and to minimize the risk of friendly fire. There is a central group acting as a command centre while the outlying groups offer various protective or attacking formations.

CASE STUDY 1:

The Greatest Manhunt in History – Finding Bin Laden: Part 2

As the surveillance on the house in Abbottabad continued, every ounce of information was fed back to intelligence centres in the United States to be sifted and analyzed. As a more detailed picture of the house was constructed, the more mysterious it looked. The false walls and entrances were designed to baffle anyone who should try to enter. All this trouble implied that this was the home of a very important person.

The President of the United States contributed to the decision that this should be a Special Forces operation and that the target should be positively identified. It was now over to Joint Special Operations Command (JSOC), part of United States Special Operations Command (USSOCOM) to find and terminate the most wanted man in American history.

Although US forces made sure of al-Zarqawi at the end of that manhunt by dropping several bombs on the house where he was located, with regard to Osama bin Laden, the President of the United States wanted to make sure of his man; he knew that if the house were bombed, it might be impossible to determine whether bin Laden had actually been inside.

SEAL Team 6

The President had confidence in the capacity of US Special Forces and in particular SEAL Team 6, or United States Naval Special Warfare Development Group, usually known as DEVGRU, to bring this off. One of the reasons for this confidence was the successful rescue by SEAL Team 6 of Captain Richard Phillips from Somali pirates in 2009. Despite having a gun held to his head, Phillips was freed unharmed because SEAL snipers killed all three pirates simultaneously with sniper rifles, despite the fact that they were on a boat about 30m (100ft) away.

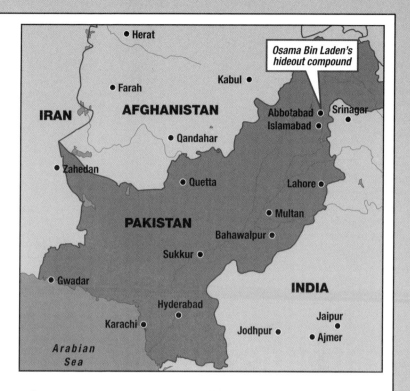

Osama Bin Laden's hideout compound

Once the go-ahead had been given and the target was known, the special operations forces engaged in a series of precise rehearsals that even included building a replica of the house where bin Laden was now almost certainly hiding. Training was carried out repeatedly at night and every contingency was explored. The key to special operations is leaving nothing to chance, although

Bin Laden's compound was located in Abbottabad, North-West Pakistan.

not every aspect of what they might come across could be predicted.

As zero-hour approached, information from satellites was rigorously examined, partly to try to ascertain that when the helicopters appeared over Pakistani territory without permission and the Navy

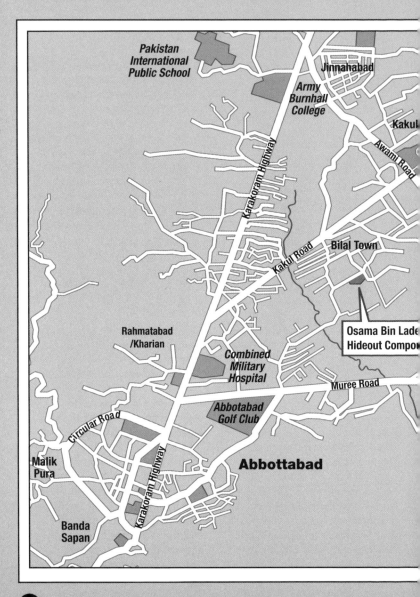

SEALs went in the target was actually present. Some imagery had revealed a man walking around the compound and, although it was not certain that it was bin Laden, it seemed likely. There was no other means of gaining confirmation without doing something that might have alerted the occupants to the possibility of a raid.

As the probability rose, some of the highest-ranking US armed forces officers and politicians gathered in a situation room in the White House. The commander of the operation, based in Afghanistan, was Vice-Admiral William McRaven, head of Joint Special Forces Command.

Near-disaster

At 1.15 a.m. on 1 May 2011, two Black Hawk MH-60 stealth helicopters took off from Bagram airbase. They headed towards Jalalabad, where they were joined by two Chinook MH-47 helicopters that carried both a back-up team as well as extra supplies. The stealth characteristics of the Black Hawk helicopters meant they were able to cross the Pakistani border undetected. This was fortunate

Bin Laden's compound was on the outskirts of town, set on an imposing hilltop.

Bin Laden's Compound

As SEAL Team 6 attacked the compound, one Black Hawk helicopter crashed outside the compound wall. Despite this, the momentum of the attack was maintained.

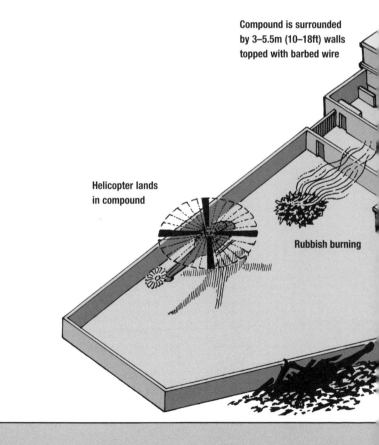

Compound is surrounded by 3–5.5m (10–18ft) walls topped with barbed wire

Helicopter lands in compound

Rubbish burning

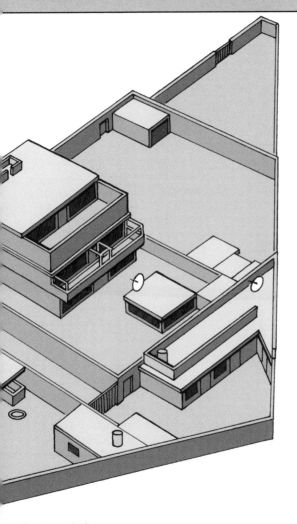

Helicopter crash site

since the US helicopters were entering the air space of a foreign power without prior permission.

Everything was going according to plan until the spectre of failure loomed out of the inky blackness as the engine died on one of the helicopters. The pilot managed to skilfully lower it to the ground without loss of life but this was a major reverse. The spectres of Desert One in Iran and of *Black Hawk Down* also loomed but SEAL Team 6 were having none of that. These men had not gone through Hell Week and all that US Navy SEAL training could throw at them to give up in the face of a mishap like this. The plan had been for one helicopter complement to fast-rope to the ground but that was no longer an option. With the helicopter inside the compound and another landing outside, the SEALs made their assault, using night-vision devices and carrying AR-15 assault rifles or Heckler & Koch 416 carbines. It is said that the team was also accompanied by a military dog for search, warning and explosive-detection.

The SEALs blasted their way through any locked doors and also walls until they were in the main residence. They met resistance from the courier al-Kuwaiti, armed with an AK-47. He was eventually killed after an exchange of fire with the SEALs.

Bin Laden Eliminated

The SEALs then worked their way up to the third floor, where they encountered Osama bin Laden himself. Although one of his wives tried to shield him, she was shot in the leg and bin Laden himself was then shot. The manhunt was over and all that remained was to take away bin Laden's body and all of his electronic equipment, including laptops. Bin Laden's body was taken on board a US aircraft carrier and buried at sea on 2 May 2011.

The manhunt for Osama bin Laden had lasted since 11 September 2001 but had ultimately been successful. During those 10 years, many lessons had been learned, technology had been developed and perfected, and methods of interrogation refined. Special Forces units had become even more focused and determined than before and their interaction with intelligence agencies both at home and on the ground almost seamless. The unblinking eye of the counter-terrorism units was now seen to pose a formidable obstacle and even a threat to the very existence of terrorist organizations.

Timeline

August 2010: Sheikh Abu Ahmed al-Kuwaiti tracked by
  surveillance teams from Peshawar to a compound and
  house in Abbottabad, in the Khyber Pakhtunkhwa province
  of Pakistan. The house is thought to have been built to hide
  Osama bin Laden and his family.

March 2011: Over the course of five national security meetings
  President Obama irons out the details for a strike on the
  house. The President rejects the original proposal to bomb
  the compound without more proof. He wants proof that bin
  Laden is dead, not a pile of rubble. The US Navy SEALs hold
  two rehearsals to prepare.

29 April 2011: 8.20 a.m. President Obama gives orders for the CIA
  and military Special Forces to strike.

1 May 2011: Bin Laden is shot in the head by US Special Forces
  during a firefight. President Obama announces the death of
  Osama Bin Laden. His body is flown to the USS *Carl Vinson*
  and then buried at sea.

Whether you are the hunter or the hunted it is vital to defend yourself in a threatening situation. Special Forces personnel operate in an environment where extreme violence can erupt at any given time. They usually carry weapons but these can malfunction, run out of ammunition or be dropped.

Fighting for Survival

Improvized weapons can be grabbed from the ground or the surroundings – it is possible to do a lot of damage with a rock, a stick, a spanner or a fire extinguisher but in a remote destination and where all else has failed, unarmed combat skills come into play, you may have to revert back to your own resources and use your own body for defense. Knowing how to deal with an attempted knife or gun attack can save lives. The key principle of unarmed combat is the intent to do as much damage to the opponent as possible in the shortest time. There is no room for fair play, and dirty tricks are in no way dishonourable. Indeed, they represent a shortcut to victory and possibly the only chance of survival.

. . . .

Officers involved in manhunts must be highly trained in the art of unarmed combat. They may be at risk of an ambush where they need to be able to fight back.

The Special Forces are susceptible to knife and gun attacks during the course of a manhunt so training to deal with these in an unarmed situation is essential and could be life-saving.

Appendix: Unarmed Combat

Knife attack

A knife attack is arguably more difficult to counter than a firearm or any other weapon attack. This is because a conventional defence against an open blade may in itself lead to a serious injury. For example, when attempting to parry the knife arm, the defender's arm could be cut in the process. Also, even if that move is successful, a serious cut could be made when either the defender or assailant draws away.

The priority for the defender, therefore, is to keep the most sensitive and vulnerable parts of their body out of reach of the assailant, to disable the knife-wielding arm if at all possible and to focus on delivering a crippling blow to the assailant that will put them out of action.

Defence Training

In order to be able to carry out effective defences against attacks, whether it be a backhand slash, a forehand slash, an overhand stab, an upward stab or a knife-to-throat attack, specific training must be given and practised.

Merely reading about a defence technique and attempting to memorize it will not be sufficient in the confusion of a real attack. No technique should be considered which involves some complex martial arts manoeuvre and which

implies that the assailant is so impressed by the manoeuvre that they will just stand and watch without doing anything. Defences against weapons require lightning-fast movements and reactions and they must be done as if by instinct.

The defence may involve a certain amount of creativity on the spot because the assailant is unlikely to have read the script and is unlikely to behave in a predictable way. If the manoeuvre is untidy, it does not matter so long as it is effective. When trying to save your life, you are entitled to try anything.

Basic Principles

However, it is worth being aware of certain principles when dealing with a knife assault. These include controlling the hand holding the knife as early as possible; putting the assailant out of action with a decisive counter-attack with legs or arms; using whatever weapons may be available, such as stones, lengths of wood or metal, bottles, sand or dirt or anything else that comes to hand which may be either temporarily or permanently disable the assailant. Self-defence should always be proportionate to the threat you encounter. If someone is attacking you with a knife, they are almost certainly trying to kill or maim you and therefore you are entitled to put a severe defence and counter-attack.

Backhand Slashing Attack

A backhand slash can be jammed by pushing the opponent's arm against his body. This immobilizes the weapon long enough to launch a counterattack. Pressure must be maintained, however; the opponent will try to step back to clear his weapon.

Knife to Throat Threat

It is absolutely vital to prevent the knife from cutting, so it must be immobilized or held away from the throat throughout any defence. The soldier achieves this by pulling the knife arm down and away from his throat (B), then rolls his shoulder forwards and down (C), dragging the opponent over to fall heavily in front of him (D and E). Finishing strikes to the head are then delivered (F). The knife arm is held throughout.

A

B

Gun attack

There are obvious limitations in defending yourself against a firearm as by their nature firearms can be used fromconsiderable distances. If being fired at from a distance and if you are unarmed, getting behind cover is the immediate priority, followed probably by getting out of the area and out of range while remaining under cover.

Defence Moves

If you are being threatened with a firearm at close quarters there are certain movements which may save your life if you believe you are in danger of being shot. As ever in countering any threat from a weapon, the defence needs to be swift and decisive if it is going to be effective. If you are being threatened by someone holding a long-barrelled weapon such as an assault rifle and the barrel of the weapon is within reach, one defence is to step forward and shove the barrel of the weapon aside and catch the barrel underneath the right armpit so it cannot be moved. Then you can disable the assailant by punching them in either the face or groin before taking control of the weapon and making your escape.

Some of the defences against hand-gun threats are illustrated in this chapter, including a defence against a gun placed high against the head and a defence for a threat to the lower back. It goes without saying that both moves have to be lightning quick in order to prevent the assailant from pulling the trigger. In both cases the assailant should be disarmed. Both of these movements and others should be practised if they are to be effective in reality.

Level of Threat

It is also important to consider the real level of threat when confronted by someone with a gun. If the assailant is merely using a gun to coerce you to do something, such as handing over a wallet, it is better to comply rather than risk a confrontation which may end in death or injury. In a military scenario, an enemy soldier may try to take someone prisoner with a weapon and not intend to kill them, in which case it is a matter of judgment whether to attempt to disarm the enemy soldier and risk being shot or to wait for another opportunity for escape. The manoeuvres described in this chapter, therefore, are mostly intended for situations where there could be a direct threat to your life if you do not do something. It cannot be over-emphasised, however, that whereas a defence may involve a movement of your whole body, however rapid, the assailant has only to pull their index finger on a trigger to either kill or disable you.

Weapon Disarm

Twisting a weapon out of the hand is a common component of military disarming techniques. Once the wrist reaches the limit of its movement the weapon can be levered free. In this case the weapon is gripped by the barrel, ensuring that it does not point in a dangerous direction.

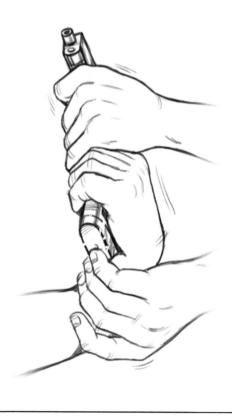

High Rear Handgun Threat

The soldier turns suddenly, knocking the weapon aside and controlling it by wrapping the weapon arm with his own. The muzzle is past him and thus not an immediate threat **(B)**. He follows up with an elbow strike to the face, tipping the opponent's head back and unbalancing him **(C)**, and hooks away his foot **(D)**. Still keeping the weapon immobilized he uses a knee-drop onto the opponent's body and delivers strikes to the head **(E)**.

A

B

C

D

E

Low Rear Handgun Threat

The soldier turns and sweeps his arm across his body, moving the weapon aside (A). It is immobilized by wrapping the arm (B). The soldier follows up any way he can. In this example he attacks the eyes, breaking the opponent's balance and tipping his head back (C). This exposes the groin to a knee strike.

A

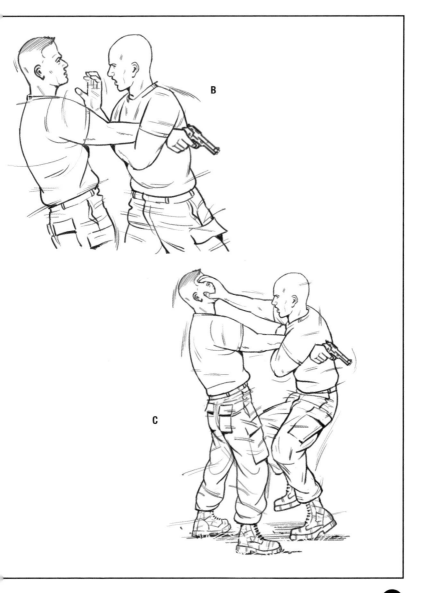

B

C

GLOSSARY

ambush – a sudden attack made from a concealed position.

bearing – the compass direction from your position to a landmark or destination.

bergen – a large backpack for carrying survival supplies.

calorie – the amount of heat required to raise the temperature of 1 gram of water by 1° Celsius.

collateral damage – damage not planned or expected to occur, e.g., civilian casualties in military operations, or an evader being caught up in fighting between two sides.

compromise – the capture of an escaped soldier, often resulting in return to captivity, further aggressive treatment and even death.

coniferous – denotes an evergreen tree with cones and needle-like leaves.

contour – a line on a map joining points of equal elevation.

coordinates – a pair of numbers and/or letters that describe a unique geographic position.

course – the route or path between two points.

deadfall trap – a trap designed to kill an animal by dropping a heavy weight on it.

dehydration – in a person, a significant loss of body fluids that are not replaced by fluid intake.

deviation – any error introduced into a compass reading by the presence of nearby iron or steel objects, magnets or electrical currents.

dysentery – a chronic diarrhoeal illness that can lead to severe dehydration and, ultimately, death.

ECCM – Electronic Counter-Countermeasures; attempts to reduce the effect of electronic countermeasures by jamming or blocking electronic signals.

elevation – height above mean sea level.

fats – natural oily substances which, in humans, are derived from food and deposited in subcutaneous layers and around some major organs.

GPS – Global Positioning Satellite; refers to the navigational satellites orbiting the Earth, which a GPS receiver utilizes to determine its exact position of longitude and latitude.

grid – the horizontal and vertical lines on a map that enable you to describe position; on a map they have a north–south and east–west orientation.

grid reference – a position defined in relation to a cartographic grid.

hearth – in survival fire lighting, the piece of wood on which you generate heat sufficient to ignite tinder.

hyperthermia – a condition in which the body temperature rises to a dangerously high level. Also known as heat-stroke.

hypothermia – a condition in which the body temperature falls to a dangerously low level. Also known as exposure.

IED – Improvised Explosive Device

insurgent – a person who militarily rebels against a political party or civil authority.

iodine – a chemical element that has a use in water purification.

JDAM – Joint Direct Attack Munitions; a kit that converts a bomb with no guidance system into a precision-guided munition.

kindling – small pieces of dry material, usually thin twigs, added to ignited tinder to develop a fire.

latitude – a measure of distance north or south of the equator.

layering – in survival clothing, refers to the principle of wearing multiple thin layers of clothing to control heat retention

longitude – a measure of distance east of west of the prime meridian.

lure – anything used in fishing or hunting that tempts prey into a trap or particular location.

magnetic north – the direction of the magnetic North Pole.

potassium permanganate – a chemical that can be used to sterilize water

PTSD – Post-Traumatic Stress Disorder; a severe anxiety disorder, sometimes experienced by soldiers after psychologically traumatic events, such as capture or imprisonment.

quarry– in tracking, the animal or human that is being hunted or pursued.

RoE – Rules of Engagement, which address where, when, how and against whom military force can be used.

satellite geometry – the arrangement of satellites in the sky above a GPS receiver as it tries to compute its position.

selous scouts – a special forces regiment of the Rhodesian Army which operated from 1973 until 1980.

sign – a term used by trackers to denote any disturbance in the environment that indicates the previous passing of a human or animal.

smoking – the process of drying out food over a smoky fire, to increase the food's storage life.

solar still – a device that traps moisture from the soil under a plastic sheet, this condensing out into drinkable water.

stalking – in tracking, the art of moving silently and stealthily so as not to alert the quarry to your presence.

stealth – the act or characteristic of moving with extreme care and quietness, so as to avoid detection.

temperate – any climate characterized by mild temperatures.

tinder – small pieces of light and dry material that are very easily ignited and are used to initiate a fire.

track – a line of sign that indicates the route of an animal or human quarry through the environment.

tracking – the pursuit of an animal or human quarry by observing and following the sign they have left behind. See also sign.

tracking stick – used to provide easy measurement of tracks across a number of planes.

trailing – another word for tracking

transit – an imaginary straight line extended through two landmarks and used as a position line.

true north – the direction of the geographic north pole.

UET – Universal Edibility Test; a test to determine whether unidentified plants (not fungi) are safe for consumption.

vitamins – a group of organic compounds that are an essential part of human nutrition, though they are required in only very small doses.

Yukon stove – an advanced survival stove consisting of a chimney of mud-packed stones over a cooking pit.

INDEX

313